P9-DMC-450

DATE DUE

APR 8 1979			

100M—6-67—38809—PP&SCo.

The Gale Library of Lives and Letters
American Writers Series

WHITMAN

The Gale Library of Lives and Letters
American Writers Series

WALT WHITMAN

BY

GEORGE RICE CARPENTER

INTRODUCTION
BY
WILLIAM WHITE
Editor, Walt Whitman Review

New York
THE MACMILLAN COMPANY

REPUBLISHED BY GALE RESEARCH COMPANY, BOOK TOWER, DETROIT, 1967

COPYRIGHT, 1909,
BY THE MACMILLAN COMPANY.

Introduction copyright © 1967
GALE RESEARCH COMPANY

Library of Congress Card Number: 67-23891

Whitman: Bibliographically Speaking

"Here's the whole thing in a nutshell without adulation or apology."

This is what Horace Traubel said Walt Whitman would have remarked about George Rice Carpenter's biography of the poet when it first appeared in 1909. No one knew Whitman better than Traubel during the last few years of Whitman's life, from about 1873 until his death in 1892, as we can see from the many volumes of *With Walt Whitman in Camden*. So Traubel on Carpenter is worth listening to: "The whole thing in a nutshell. Never over and never short. Good measure and full weight. Judicial without being judicious. Cool enough for justice and warm enough for love. Carpenter knows how to handle eggs without smashing them and knows how to handle steel without smashing himself. He goes anywhere without any sort of intimation that it takes any nerve to do so."

Who is this Carpenter and what is this book?

The Macmillan Company of New York decided early in this century to expand its highly successful English Men of Letters Series, and in its "American Extension" included Ralph Waldo Emerson, John

Greenleaf Whittier, William Hickling Prescott, William Cullen Bryant, and Walt Whitman. That Whitman was in the series at all is remarkable, for he was still considered by many as the Henry Miller or the Allen Ginsberg of his day. But Harvard Professor Bliss Perry had gone a long way to make Whitman acceptable by his critical study of the author of *Leaves of Grass,* published by Houghton Mifflin of Boston in 1906.

George Rice Carpenter (1863-1909) was a well regarded Professor of Rhetoric in Columbia University, a scholar of English grammar, translator of Dante, and biographer of Longfellow and Whittier. As early as 1906 he was working on Whitman, for he wrote Traubel: "Dr. Curtis Hidden Page is kind enough to give me a message from you that you would have no objection to my going through the Whitman scrapbooks which are in your possession. You are very kind to allow me this privilege, and I hope to avail myself of it before I go abroad this autumn. I am delaying the completion of my little biography until I can go over all the material with renewed care." That he produced this "little biography" with great care is shown by its completion taking almost three years.

The reviews that greeted the book were uniformly good: one said that Carpenter placed "Whitman in the class of men who represented a new attitude, who bring a message to their brothers, a truth expressed in their lives and only incidentally through their writings"; another that this was the "clearest, plainest, and least vexatious account of Walt Whitman in print"; and many of them spoke of the readability and proportion and pleasantness of the biography.

There were several earlier books on Whitman, from the first by William Douglas O'Connor, *The Good Gray Poet: A Vindication* (1866), John Burroughs' *Notes on Walt Whitman as Poet and Person* (1867), and Dr. Richard Maurice Bucke's *Walt Whitman* (1883). They all knew their subject personally, and Whitman's own hand can be seen in their volumes— which makes them of first-hand value today. Others in contact with the poet, John Addington Symonds, William Sloane Kennedy, and Thomas Donaldson brought out further books in 1893 and 1896. The earliest scholarly biography was by an Englishman, Henry Bryan Binns in 1905, which avoided the idolatry of the "hot little prophets" (as Bliss Perry called them). The following year came the work of another idolater, Edward Carpenter, the first of Traubel's *With Walt Whitman in Camden* (five volumes have been published, with more to come), and Perry's *Walt Whitman: His Life and Work,* which was and is of considerable value but did not please Traubel (who referred to its "malignant falsities and its clownish superciliousness").

Just a few words about the avalanche of Whitman biography, criticism, and special studies in the past fifty-eight years: Emory Holloway's Pulitzer Prize-winning *Whitman: An Interpretation in Narrative* (1926), the most scholarly of all the lives; Frederik Schyberg's *Whitman* (in Danish, 1933; translated into English by Evie Allison Allen, 1951), an extraordinarily penetrating study; Henry Seidel Canby's sympathetic *Walt Whitman: An American* (1943), which he called "a biography of an inner life and of the mysterious creative processes of poetry"; Gay Wilson Allen's

The Solitary Singer: A Critical Biography of Walt Whitman (1955), the most detailed life we are likely to get in the foreseeable future; and Roger Asselineau's heavily documented two-volume interpretation, through sexual determinism, of the author and his work, *The Evolution of Walt Whitman: The Creation of a Personality* (Vol. I, 1960) and *The Creation of a Book* (Vol. II, 1962).

To return to Carpenter's little biography, which sold in 1909 for "75 cents, net; by mail, 84 cents": despite its being written long before the tremendous accumulation of knowledge about Whitman, without a definitive text of the poetry, very little of the journalism and no decent edition of Whitman's *Correspondence* (which we now have in the fine New York University Press *Collected Writings),* and even without the full acceptance of Whitman in critical and academic circles, the Columbia Professor of Rhetoric was responsible for a book so well done it is worth republishing more than a half-century later. Relying on material available to him, Carpenter has given the general reader almost as much as he needs to know of Walt Whitman's life for an appreciation of the poetry, and in the chapter on "Workman and Poet (1850-1860)" he shows how *Leaves of Grass* was a product of Whitman's sensitive and creative talent at that time and in that place.

Once more, Horace Traubel's review in the February 1909 *Conservator* of Carpenter's book deserves quoting: "Carpenter has got all the big things in this little book. He has consummately arrayed his detail so as to make his narrative most efficient for schools and for answering the first curiosity of new comers . . .

Carpenter makes no bid either in letter or spirit for institutional or social honors. He keeps his Whitman on the ground. Presents him without glorifications or disguises. The rest can be left to take care of itself."

Finally, Traubel refers to the "Walt's humanism. [Carpenter] keeps on talking of it because he knows how much it means to any adequate portrait. Walt is a rebel's man. If you are afraid of rebellion you are afraid of Walt. If you prefer conformity why dally with revolt? Cut out from [Ralph] Waldo [Emerson] and Walt their brazen defiances and you wouldn't have enough man left to furnish a decent excuse for a funeral. Carpenter puts this fact where it belongs . . . [Carpenter] grasped the Whitman situation without being distracted by moral ephemera."

Thus the appeal of George Rice Carpenter's *Walt Whitman* in 1909 and thus its continuing appeal in 1967.

William White
Editor, *Walt Whitman Review*

Wayne State University
September, 1967

CONTENTS

CHAPTER I

v

WALT WHITMAN

CHAPTER I

BOYHOOD (1819–1841)

LONG ISLAND had been the home of the Whitmans
for generations. Fish-shaped, as Whitman loved to
picture it, it stretches away from New York, running
a little to the north of east, for one hundred and
twenty-five miles, with an average breadth of about
twelve. On the north it has several fine harbours, in
the middle a ridge of low hills, on the south a scarcely
broken stretch of narrow, desolate, dangerous beach,
protecting the inner waters of a chain of bays. The
western settlements in the island were originally Dutch;
the eastern were made by the English, — Independents
of the old breed, shut off from Connecticut by the Sound,
and from New York by the sandy wilderness, but
sturdily content in their isolation. Journeying east
from New York, even as late as Whitman's childhood,
one soon passed out of the village of Brooklyn and its
outlying farms into the great Hempstead plain, un-
broken by tree, shrub, or fence, a pasture-ground for
sheep and cattle, who fattened on the coarse grass that
grew abundantly in its black but thin soil. Then, as
the mould became mixed with sand, came the "brushy
plains" of scrub oak. Forty miles of this, and, as the
sand increased in fineness and fluidity, one entered
the "pine plains," a low, irregular forest that con-

tinued to the sand dunes of the east. The railroad
did not penetrate far into the island until 1841; the
roads were bad, and communication by sea was often
hazardous. "The necessary consequence is," says an
historian of the island in 1845, "that locomotion, at
least to any distance from home, is almost unknown
on Long Island. The writer has heard men sixty
years of age say that they were never twenty miles
from the spot on which they were born; and no doubt
there are many now living who never breathed the
atmosphere of more than two towns in their lives."
Huntington, the Whitman township, lay towards the
middle of the island, forty miles east of Brooklyn,
and stretched from the beautiful many-forked northern bay, with its excellent harbours, to the salt marshes
and beaches of the south. It contained more than a
hundred square miles and was sparsely settled. The
climate was tempered by the sea air; the soil, when
fertilized by the weeds and fish of the sea, repaid care;
the life was peaceful, honest, and hearty; the inhabit-
ants were farmers who were no strangers to the sea.
And the isolation was that of a far-distant land.

Whitman is so deeply associated in our minds with
the teeming life of Manhattan that it is difficult to
realize that he was a country boy. He was born
May 31, 1819, in the hamlet of West Hills, in this
township of Huntington, Suffolk County, Long Island,
where his ancestors had lived since the middle of the
seventeenth century. Like Whittier, he sprang from
an old, permanently settled country stock, long thoroughly adapted to its environment, and now ready to
bear its unique flower and fruit.

This environment was scarcely to be differentiated

from that of New England. Huntington had been
settled in 1653 by New England colonists, and for a
century and a half its connections with the mainland
across the Sound — scarcely more than ten miles wide
at this point, from land to land — were closer than
those with Brooklyn and New York. It had been
early decided by Dutch and English commissioners
that the Dutch should not interfere with settlements
to the east of Oyster Bay, which were absolutely English in character and had been admitted as members
of the Connecticut or the New Haven Colony. In
1664, much against their will, Huntington and its
sister settlements became part of the possessions of
the Duke of York, to be governed by the hated
"Duke's laws," which did not provide for representation in a general assembly. The island became
Yorkshire, and Huntington was in the "East Riding."
The pioneers submitted with ill grace, for as an outlying member of the Connecticut Colony they had been
almost absolutely independent, and they flatly refused
to contribute to the repair of the New York fort, on
the ground that they were deprived of the liberties of
Englishmen. In 1673 the Dutch seized New York
again and laid a heavy hand on Huntington, which
refused to take any oath that would pledge it to bear
arms against Great Britain, and plainly looked to
being taken, like Easthampton, Southampton, and
Southold, under the protection of Connecticut. The
Dutch occupation, however, was brief, and the town
was forced back under the abhorred "Duke's laws."
Even after representation was granted, in 1683, its
sympathies were still with Connecticut rather than
with New York, and though it was inclined to look

with favour on the anti-aristocratic rule of Leisler, it refused to send delegates to the legislature, and did not cease to desire a fresh union with Connecticut until the fall of the Stuarts and the new colonial legislation made such a political conjunction forever out of the question.

Like the majority of the early settlers in eastern Long Island, the Whitmans were of English stock and Independents in faith. An apparently baseless tradition has connected them with Zechariah Whitman, a ruling elder and ordained teacher who emigrated from England in 1635 and lived in New Haven and Milford; but this Zechariah left no issue. Joseph, who was admitted freeman of Connecticut from Huntington in 1664, is probably the same Joseph who is referred to in the minutes of the meeting of the New Haven general court in 1655 as living in Stratford, Connecticut. He was apparently a man of solid ability and character, and the carefully preserved records of Huntington make frequent mention of him. In 1679 Andros arbitrarily ordered him to present himself, as late constable of the town, in New York, as if to answer charges for undue independence of his Excellency's trading regulations. He was constable, grand juryman, surveyor, townsman, leather-sealer. He owned several farms; bought, sold, and exchanged land with an activity that smacks of the Yankee speculator; and he was still living in 1698. His sons appear to have been Joseph, John, Nathaniel, and Samuel, of whom we know little except that against Joseph complaint was brought in 1690 by Henry Whitney for " stealing his daughter's affections contrary to her mother's mind and using unlawful means

to obtain his daughter's love." The testimony cited
seems to show that Joseph was a " good lad," though
scarcely yet settled in life. Here tradition fails; but
from among the increasing number of the Whitmans
whom the records show, one certainly moved from the
old "town spot" to a farm in the hills (West Hills),
a little to the south, henceforth to be the home of that
branch of the family, and his son Nehemiah was the
father of Jesse, whom we know to have been Walt
Whitman's grandfather.

Whatever may be the truth as to the exact geneal-
ogy, the Whitmans were old Huntington settlers, well
known in their district, and it is almost inconceivable
that they should have married otherwise than among
their neighbours, who were virtually all of similar
blood. The lady irregularly wooed by the second
Joseph was either a Whitney or a Ketchum, both
familiar names in the early records, and Jesse married
a Brush, a name which, since the foundation of the
settlement, had been written in close connection with
that of his ancestors.

And there these pioneers lived out their lives with
their fellows, in a region peculiarly fitted to breed
quiet and stalwart independence. At first they dwelt
on the old "town spot," with its forts and watch-
houses and trainbands, raising what crops they could,
clearing the ground, building houses and barns, plant-
ing orchards, making timber and clapboards. They
had matchlock guns, wooden ploughshares tipped with
iron, and ox carts. The women ground the corn. Before the older generation died the village was in order.
There were saw-mills and grist-mills, tanneries, brick
yards, and docks, a church and a school; the whale-

boats plied to and fro on the Sound, and smart little
vessels bore barrel staves and pork to the West Indies,
returning with sugar, molasses, and rum.   Cattle had
increased, each bearing the crop of its owner, duly
registered in the town records.   The soil proved fairly
fertile, the Indians gave little trouble, the salt marshes
yielded hay in abundance, and the colonists spread
themselves slowly out over their district, apportion-
ing the lands in their semi-socialistic fashion.   Of
the neighbouring counties they knew little.   New
York was forty miles away, over bad roads, and its
authority was light.   They lived quietly in peace and
independence — the typical life of the Anglo-Saxon
community.   Even religion was not a disturbing fac-
tor, as the records show, for these were no zealots but
plain-living country farmers and sea-traders.

The Revolution told heavily on them.   The battle
of Long Island cut them off from aid, British squadron after squadron anchored in the great harbour, and
troops were quartered on them,— Erskine's, Tarleton's,
and Tryon's men and Hessians, insolent and brutal.
Huntington was easy of access by sea, and the troops
there could collect provisions for the New York garri-
son and at the same time keep an eye on the Connecticut rebels.   The local militia, in which Jesse Whitman
served, were forced to work on fortifications and (under
that imperious renegade Yankee, Benjamin Thompson,
later Count Rumford) to share in demolishing their
church and in building, in the midst of the burying
place on the hill, the hated Fort " Golgotha," using in
the construction of the ovens the tombstones of their
fathers.   The young men waylaid little troops of
British soldiers, and spies came and went from Con-

necticut, among them Nathan Hale, who was captured
on the harbour shore. The township was desolated by
a bitter guerilla warfare, made more bitter still,
shame to say, by bands of marauders who robbed both
parties.

The Revolution over, the quiet and prosperous life
began again, scarcely broken by the flurry of excitement caused by the War of 1812. The region was still
remote. Eastward and westward the roads were bad,
and Huntington brooded in the isolation of the mid-
island. It was New England in its independence and
self-reliance, more free even than Connecticut from
the presence of the aristocratic ideal in any shape;
but unlike New England in the absence of theoretic
influences, of morbid religious and emotional analysis,
of intense ambition for learning or godliness or wealth,
— an almost ideal community, it would seem, where
life was sane and healthy, and naught disturbed the
growth of all the peaceful and democratic virtues.

The Whitmans, the biographers tell us, were a sturdy
race; "solid, tall, strong-framed, long-lived, moderate
of speech, friendly, fond of their land and of horses
and cattle, sluggish in their passions but fearful when
once started," Dr. Bucke records. Their wives were
likely to be women of strong character, also, if we
judge from Mr. Burroughs' statement that Nehemiah's
wife, the great-grandmother, " was a large, swarthy
woman, who smoked tobacco, rode on horseback
like a man, managed the most vicious horse, and
becoming a widow later in life, went forth every day
over her farm-lands, frequently in the saddle, direct-
ing the labor of her slaves." The grandfather, Jesse,
however, married a woman of gentler type, Hannah

Brush, a schoolmistress. Whitman's mother was Louisa, daughter of Major Cornelius Van Velsor, a Dutch farmer at Cold Spring Harbour, three or four miles from West Hills, and of Amy (Naomi) Williams, his wife, daughter of Captain Williams, a trader to the West Indies. The Williamses were seafaring folk and of Quaker sympathies, and Whitman describes his grandmother as belonging to the Society of Friends, though it would seem that she was not technically a member of it. " The Van Velsors," says Dr. Bucke, were " fond of horses, the raising of which from blooded stock was a part of their occupation, and Louisa when young was herself a daring and spirited rider. As a woman and mother she was of marked spiritual and intuitive nature, remarkably healthy and strong, had a kind, generous heart, good sense, and a cheerful and even temper."

The father, Walter Whitman, Senior, passed his childhood on the farm at West Hills, and was as a lad apprenticed as a carpenter in New York, — the first of his line, apparently, to pass into the outer world. " His business," says Dr. Bucke, " for many years extended into various parts of Long Island. He was a large, quiet, serious man, very kind to children and animals, and a good citizen, neighbour, and parent. Not a few of his barn and house frames, with their seasoned timber and careful braces and joists, are still standing (1883) in Suffolk and Queen's counties and in Brooklyn, strong and plumb as ever."

The boy spent his early years on the farm. The family moved to Brooklyn when he was four, but for a long time afterwards he apparently passed a good part of each year with his grandmothers, and it was

not until he was a man grown that he stepped definitely out of the old Long Island country life. His
childhood's impressions he has recorded in *There was
a Child went Forth*, in *Out of the Cradle endlessly
Rocking*, and in *Specimen Days*. He was a quiet,
thoughtful, but active youth, showing genius in no
point, but, as we can see now, capable of very deep
impressions, of which he did not until middle life
attempt analysis. In the first-mentioned poem he
touches only on the sights and sounds that thus became
part of him : —

> " The early lilacs became part of this child,
>   And grass and white and red morning-glories, and white and
>   red clover, and the song of the phœbe-bird,
>   And the Third-month lambs, and the sow's pink-faint litter,
>   and the mare's foal and the cow's calf,
>   And the noisy brood of the barn-yard, or by the mire of the
>   pond-side,
>   And the fish suspending themselves so curiously below there,
>   and the beautiful curious liquid,
>   And the water-plants with their graceful flat heads, all be-
>   came part of him."

In the second he sings a reminiscence : —

> " For more than once dimly down to the beach gliding,
>   Silent, avoiding the moonbeams, blending myself with the
>   shadows,
>   Recalling now the obscure shapes, the echoes, the sounds and
>   sights after their sorts,
>   The white arms out in the breakers tirelessly tossing,
>   I, with bare feet, a child, the wind wafting my hair,
>   Listen'd long and long "

to the song of a bird, vainly and lovingly calling its
dead mate, and to the melodious hissing of the sea.

It was at that hour, it seemed to him in later years, that the poet was born in him, and he was never to forget those two voices, the desolate bird that sang of love and the sea that whispered of death.

In his prose reminiscences he entered more fully into detail, recalling the "wooded, hilly, healthy surroundings," the broad and beautiful farm lands, the famous apple orchard, the "stately grove of tall, vigorous black walnuts, beautiful, Apollo-like," and the old Van Velsor homestead, — "the vast kitchen and ample fireplace and the sitting-room adjoining, the plain furniture, the meals, the house full of merry people, my grandmother Amy's sweet old face in its Quaker cap, my grandfather 'the Major,' jovial, red, stout, with sonorous voice and characteristic physiognomy." He remembered vividly also his associations with the picturesque inlets of the North Shore and the great bays and beaches of the South Shore, and its long list of tragic wrecks, with the traditions of which he was familiar as a boy and of one or two of which he was almost an observer. As a lad he often went to gather sea-gulls' eggs in summer, and in winter to fish on the frozen waters of the shallow bays, "with hand-sled, axe and eel-spear, after messes of eels. We would cut holes in the ice, sometimes striking quite an eel-bonanza, and filling our baskets with great, fat, sweet, white-meated fellows. The scenes, the ice, drawing the hand-sled, cutting holes, spearing the eels, etc., were of course just such fun as is dearest to boyhood." He knew, too, the "blue-fishers and sea-bass takers" of the eastern end of the island; on Montauk peninsula, the "strange, unkempt, half-barbarous herdsmen" and the few remaining Indians and half-breeds;

in the middle of the island, the spreading, prairie-
like Hempstead plains, with their thousands of cattle,
and could recall in fancy " the interminable cow pro-
cessions," as they found their way home at nightfall,
"and hear the music of the tin and copper bells
clanking far and near, and breathe the cool of the
sweet and slightly aromatic evening air, and note the
sunset."

"Through the same region of the island," he continues,
"but further east, extended wide central tracts of pine and
scrub-oak, (charcoal was largely made here,) monotonous and
sterile. But many a good day or half-day did I have, wandering through those solitary cross-roads, inhaling the peculiar
and wild aroma. Here, and all along the island and its shores,
I spent [at] intervals many years, all seasons, sometimes riding,
sometimes boating, but generally afoot, (I was always then a
good walker,) absorbing fields, shores, marine incidents, characters, the bay-men, farmers, pilots — always had a plentiful
acquaintance with the latter, and with fishermen — went every
summer on sailing trips — always liked the bare sea-beach,
south side, and have some of my happiest hours on it to this
day. As I write, the whole experience comes back to me after
the lapse of forty and more years — the soothing rustle of the
waves, and the saline smell — boyhood's times, the clam-dig-
ging, barefoot, and with trousers roll'd up — hauling down the
creek — the perfume of the sedge-meadows — the hay-boat, and
the chowder and fishing excursions."

The Brooklyn in which Whitman found himself as
a boy was not the great city of to-day, though it was
at the very beginning of its rapid development. The
population of the whole township in 1824 was only
about nine thousand, and that of the village itself
scarcely over seven thousand. The houses were
mainly clustered around the Old (Fulton) Ferry,
below the abrupt rise which is now the Heights and

was then Clover Hill. The older Dutch houses were
quaintly built of stone or with small imported Hol-
land bricks, and among them the pert-looking Yankee
frame edifices stood out as rude intruders. " Yet one
and all," says Mr. Stiles, the historian of the city,
" wore an unpretentious and neighborly look, under
the drooping shadows of the noble elms with which
the city abounded." The streets were unpaved, un-
lighted, without sidewalks, and those who went abroad
at night must pick their way by the light of their own
lanterns through streets often well-nigh impassable
from mud and mire. There were wharves and storehouses, slaughtering-houses, distilleries, ropewalks,
and various manufactories. The mail went once a
day to New York.

The antiquarians have patiently restored the old
village, street by street, house by house, family by
family, and he who pores over their works may imagine how it struck the eyes of the country lad. It was
a step in his preparation for the larger world, a friendly
little spot where every one knew everybody and where
he quietly grew to greater knowledge of mankind. It
was a quaint place, too, full of strange names and
strange characters, all good to teach a lad the many-
sidedness of life. He could see his townsfolk in 1829,
as Furman records in his manuscript notes, still dig-
ging for Captain Kidd's money; and he knew, no doubt,
the whole picturesque mixture of Dutch and Hugue-
not and English life, even to Het Dorp, the town plot
of Bushwick, reluctantly giving up its Dutch character, and Greenpoint, unyielding in its old Dutch ways;
though his earliest memories were of the ferries, —
how he was petted by the gatekeepers and deck hands,

and "the horses that seem'd to me so queer as they
trudg'd around the central houses of the boats, making the water-power." And now and then he had a
glimpse of the greater outer world, as when, on the
occasion of the laying of a corner-stone, he found himself, a child of five, close to Lafayette, who gave him
a kiss and set him down in a safer place in the throng.

In Brooklyn, then just beginning to stir with new
life, the father plied his trade, and built house after
house for himself, each of which was successively
mortgaged and eventually lost. The children were
Jesse, born in 1818; Walter,[1] fifteen months younger;
Mary Elizabeth, 1821; Louisa, 1823; an unnamed in-
fant, who lived only a few months, 1825; Andrew
Jackson, 1827; George Washington, 1829; Thomas
Jefferson, 1833; and Edward, crippled in body and
weak of mind, 1835. With his brothers and sisters
Walt, it should be said in passing, was throughout his
life on terms of intimacy and affection. Of his relations with his father we hear little, and it may be sur-
mised that from the outset the hard-working, serious,
practical man found it difficult to understand a lad
whose wayward, emotional temperament grew with
his years, and who lacked the desire to turn his
pennies to the best account. For sympathy and understanding the child must have instinctively turned
then, as he did his whole life long, to his mother, a
remarkable woman, whose calm good sense, never

---

[1] "At home, through infancy and boyhood, he was always
called ' Walt,' to distinguish him from his father ' Walter,' and
the short name has always been used for him by his relatives
and friends" (Dr. Bucke). In his manhood he deliberately
adopted the shorter name.

failing equanimity, and insight into the essentials of life and character he never ceased to praise.

The family was large and its needs were imperative, and the lad was early set to work. He had attended the public schools for several years, and in 1831, as a lad of twelve, he was engaged in a lawyer's office, where he had " a nice desk and window-nook " to himself. One of his employers helped him with his handwriting and composition, and "(the signal event of my life up to that time) subscribed for me to a big circulating library. For a time I now revell'd in romance-reading of all kinds; first, the *Arabian Nights*, all the volumes, an amazing treat. Then, with sorties in very many other directions, took in Walter Scott's novels, one after another, and his poetry." He left this friendly haven for a similar position in a doctor's office; and then, in 1833, when his family moved back to the country again, he began life in earnest as a printer's apprentice in the office of the *Long Island Patriot*, a weekly paper of very limited circulation, printed by hand on an old-fashioned wooden press. Whitman recalled pleasantly his life there: " An old printer in the house, William Hartshorne, a revolutionary character, who had seen Washington, was a special friend of mine, and I had many a talk with him about long-past times. The apprentices, including myself, boarded with his granddaughter. I used occasionally to go out riding with the boss, who was very kind to us." Later, in 1834 or 1835, he was a compositor on the *Long Island Star*, another weekly or semi-weekly paper, the editor of which afterward characterized him facetiously as a lazy lad — too lazy to shake even with an ague. Like many a printer, he

had a taste for literary composition. Several "senti-
mental bits " had appeared in the *Patriot*, and " a piece
or two in George P. Morris's then celebrated and fashionable *Mirror*, of New York City. I remember with
what half-suppressed excitement I used to watch for
the big, fat, red-faced, slow-moving, very old English
carrier who distributed the *Mirror* in Brooklyn; and
when I got one, opening and cutting the leaves with
trembling fingers. How it made my heart double-beat
to see *my piece* on the pretty paper in nice type."

Whitman's love for reading, his taste for writing,
his sound training as a compositor, and his native
genius for friendship, combined to give him a bent for
teaching, and in 1836 and 1837, after working, according to his own account, in printing-offices in New
York, he began this new profession as a country peda-
gogue at Babylon, on the south shore of the island.
He is remembered as a big, earnest, quiet fellow,
neatly dressed, black-haired and fresh-faced, and a
moderately good teacher, though kindly and uncon-
ventional in his methods of discipline as contrasted
with the somewhat brutal methods of the day. His
pupils were partly girls, but he showed no senti-
mental tendencies, and his friendships were mostly
with his elders.

Teaching led naturally to journalism, and in 1838
we find him back in his own " beautiful town of Huntington," where he had been encouraged to start a paper
which he called the *Long Islander*. " I bought a press
and types," he relates, " hired some little help, but
did most of the work myself, including the press-
work. Everything seem'd turning out well; (only
my own restlessness prevented my gradually estab-

lishing a permanent property there.) I bought a good
horse, and every week went all round the country
serving my papers, devoting one day and night to it.
I never had happier jaunts — going over to south side,
to Babylon, down the south road, across to Smithtown
and Comac, and back home. The experience of those
jaunts, the dear old-fashion'd farmers and their wives,
the stops by the hay-fields, the hospitality, nice dinners, occasional evenings, the girls, the rides through
the brush, and the smell from the dale of the south
woods, come up in my memory to this day."

From journalism he shifted restlessly back to
teaching again, in 1839–1841, at Babylon, in Jamaica
Academy, and elsewhere. And now we hear of him
as a debater in several local societies, and as a public
speaker on political questions. New ideas were ob-
truding themselves into his slow-growing mind, and
he was from the outset more or less of a radical. He
was an abolitionist, a teetotaler, and opposed to capital punishment — three doctrines which he held in
common with Whittier, the Massachusetts country
boy and young journalist and politician, whose early
career had many points of similarity with his. In
the campaign of 1840 he spoke often for Van Buren,
the Democratic nominee, and it was plain that the
impulse to self-expression, whether by teaching, by
writing, or by speaking, was rooting itself deeply in
his heart.

Few facts have been published that throw any special
light upon his state of mind in this period. His mother
relates that he was a very good but a very strange
boy. He once, in later life, spoke of his boyhood as
restless and unhappy. We may perhaps surmise that,

in spite of his robust appearance and his constitutional indolence, he was nervously highly impressionable. He speaks himself of the Whitman stubbornness of mind, and various hints would indicate that he was disposed to find his own way, and to persist in it, and that the many and various impulses of youth, imperfectly coördinated, gave him a vague unrest until he had worked out, in his own slow-going fashion, their destined combination.

At all events, it was a good start in life, and one typical of the Middle States, where the great formative and stimulating influences of education and religion were weaker than in New England. His technical learning had been slight, but he had been made free of the world of books and of men; and his fate lay in his own hands. For a college education he had apparently no ambition. Nor was religion a pressing matter with him. His father was fond of hearing Elias Hicks preach, and as a boy Whitman was deeply moved by one of the last sermons of the old prophet of the inner light; but there was nothing to urge the lad to a keen feeling of the need of salvation or to a desire for a spiritual life. Promptings toward self-aggrandizement or self-sacrifice were alike absent. He was a healthy, hearty, well-balanced youth, temperate, free from vicious habits, fond of out-door life, with such education in books as all may have, and such education in life as everybody gets who learns a trade and who knows the country and the city. Such a youth, slow-evolving, unawakened, easy-going, was the normal American boy, whom ambition, personal charm, or force of character might later lead to great distinction or who might live and die a quiet and ordinary citizen.

c

CHAPTER II

FOR the following decade the biographer of Whitman is almost without significant data. We may trace roughly the outward course of Whitman's life, but we lack the knowledge of his inner life that would alone make these facts of importance. No definite act or recorded syllable of his or of others serves to reveal any of the slow stages by which he must have been steadily growing towards his greater self. In the absence of information that is vitally significant, we can only state the few facts of which record is preserved, describe briefly his somewhat colourless writing during this period, and add whatever conjectures we can reasonably make as to the trend of his mind and his art.

In 1841 Whitman was a compositor in the office of the *New World*, and a little later he was editor successively for a few months of the *Aurora* and the *Tattler*, newspapers of which we know nothing more than the names, and perhaps of one or two other inconspicuous or short-lived journals. In 1842 he wrote a short novel, *Franklin Evans*, and between 1841 and 1848 he contributed not only to the columns of various newspapers, but to the pages of the *Democratic Review*, the *Broadway Journal*, the *American Review*, and a number of other periodicals.

The novitiate of miscellaneous writing past, we find
Whitman in 1846, in a more responsible position, as
editor of the Brooklyn *Daily Eagle*, and living with
his father and mother in Brooklyn. His opinions
with regard to slavery and free soil, however, gave
offence to some influential readers and to the owners,
and with characteristic indifference he relinquished
the post in 1847 or early in 1848. Just at that time
he met one evening, in the lobby of the old Broadway
Theatre, a Southern gentleman who was starting a
daily paper in New Orleans, and, though that was
their first acquaintance, it was formally agreed after
fifteen minutes' talk that Whitman should be one of
his staff, and two hundred dollars was paid to bind
the contract and to cover Whitman's travelling expenses. A few days later he was on his leisurely
way southward, through Pennsylvania and Virginia,
across the Alleghanies, and by steamer from Wheel-
ing down the Ohio and the Mississippi. He was
accompanied by his brother "Jeff," a boy of fifteen,
who was to work in the printing-office.

The first issue of the *Crescent*, a four-paged paper
of a type familiar at that day, appeared March 6,
1848, and contained Whitman's *Sailing the Mississippi
at Midnight*. His duties were apparently those
of a general factotum: he wrote editorials, news items,
or, more frequently, descriptive articles on the hotels,
bar-rooms, and levee front, and the people whom he
found there. In his old age, writing for the fiftieth-
year edition of the New Orleans *Picayune*, he recalled
with pleasure the varied and curious spectacle of the
old French market; the admirable coffee, the cool
"cobblers," the exquisite wines and perfect brandy,

the hours "on the crowded and bustling levees," and his "acquaintances among captains, boatmen, and other characters."

But though his situation was a pleasant one, his brother was ill and homesick, and it seemed time to move on. They therefore took passage on the *Pride of the West*, May 26, for St. Louis; they proceeded thence by the *Prairie Bird* to La Salle, by canal to Chicago, by steamer through the Lakes to Buffalo, and by way of Niagara and Albany to New York. Thereafter we hear nothing of him until 1850, when he is referred to by a brother journalist as having " lately established the *Daily Freeman* in Brooklyn, to promulgate his favourite Free Soil and other reformatory doctrines." Quite probably he had rejoined his family in Brooklyn on his return from the South.

No portrait of Whitman at this period is extant, and of his appearance we can guess only from the description of an associate of his on the *Aurora*, who remembered him many years later as " tall and graceful in appearance, neat in attire," and as " having a very pleasing and impressive eye and a cheerful, happy-looking countenance. He usually wore a frock coat and a high hat, carried a small cane, and the lapel of his coat was almost invariably ornamented with a boutonnière." In his habits of work he showed the same calm detachment that had characterized him as a youth. Reaching his office between eleven and twelve o'clock, he looked over the local papers and the exchanges. It was then his habit " to stroll down Broadway to the Battery, spending an hour or two amid the trees and enjoying the water view, returning

to the office at about two or three o'clock in the after-
noon." Small wonder that the owner of the *Aurora*
thought him "the laziest fellow who ever undertook
to edit a city paper." On the Brooklyn *Eagle* his professional habits, so the tradition runs, were much the
same. His house was a mile and a half away. "Not
only did he walk, or saunter, to and fro from the office,
but almost daily he left his desk and took a swim and
a stroll, leaving the nations to get on as they might
without his comment and advice, and often taking
one of the printers from his case for company." Such
a leisurely life, in a city where most men toil so
fiercely for fame or gain, is not to be hastily dispar-
aged. If he limited his chances of professional
success, he at least gained, by thus giving way to his
temperament, a more robust health, a broader outlook
on the world, a more hearty contentment in it, and a
more complete freedom from the ruts of conventionalism that incessant and narrow endeavour beats so
quickly into the brain. And he was reserving his
greater strength for the heavier tasks that his genius
was soon to lay upon him.

Two further characteristics of Whitman's, oddly dis-
similar, were also becoming more clearly marked, —
a fondness for solitude and a craving for companionship. In solitude he sought opportunity for meditation and for reading. In his reminiscences he says
that he "used to go off, sometimes for weeks at a
stretch, down in the country or to Long Island's sea-
shores—there in the presence of out-door influences,
I went over thoroughly the Old and New Testaments,
and absorb'd (probably to better advantage for me
than in any library or indoor room — it makes such

difference *where* you read), Shakspere, Ossian, the best translated versions I could get of Homer, Eschylus, Sophocles, the old German Nibelungen, the ancient Hindoo poems, and one or two other masterpieces, Dante's among them. As it happen'd, I read the latter mostly in an old wood. The *Iliad* (Buckley's prose version) I read first thoroughly on the peninsula of Orient, northeast end of Long Island, in a shelter'd hollow of rocks and sand, with the sea on each side." And, in another passage, he speaks of visits to Coney Island, " at that time a long, bare, unfrequented shore, which I had all to myself, and where I loved, after bathing, to race up and down the hard sand, and declaim Homer or Shakspere to the surf and seagulls by the hour."

This solitude, this communion with nature, this increasingly insistent habit of lonely meditation, lay deep at the roots of his growing genius, and it is wholly characteristic of the evolution of his special powers that we find him at first submitting himself instinctively to the influence of the great classics of old. Alone under stimulating physical influences, he first found gratification, while powerless himself to express his emotions, in reading and repeating the greatest literary records of antiquity. These he sought out unerringly. Uneducated in a sense, unacquainted with foreign languages, untrained in history and philosophy, he was yet pushing onwards toward education in a truer sense of the word. He had not the temptations of the man of university training: literature and language did not present themselves to him as an established scheme, already definitely determined, with which he was to become

familiar according to a system; the duty of understanding why masterpieces are what they are did not
lie heavy on him; philosophic and philological and
historical comments did not obtrude themselves between him and literature itself. He was free to com-
prehend, to appreciate, to absorb with reference to his
own needs alone. And, as the result showed, his
miscellaneous reading bred in him power.

His second passion was for people. The astonishing range of his acquaintance at this period, and for
many years later, has been best described by his first
biographer, Dr. Bucke : —

"He knew the hospitals, poorhouses, prisons, and their in-
mates. He passed freely in and about those parts of the city
which are inhabited by the worst characters ; he knew all their
people, and many of them knew him ; he learned to tolerate
their squalor, vice, and ignorance ; he saw the good (often
much more than the self-righteous think) and the bad that was
in them, and what there was to excuse and justify their lives.
It is said that these people, even the worst of them, while entire strangers to Walt Whitman, quite invariably received him
without discourtesy and treated him well. Perhaps only those
who have known the man personally, and have felt the peculiar
magnetism of his presence, can fully understand this. Many of
the worst of those characters became singularly attached to him.
He knew and was sociable with the man that sold peanuts at
the corner, and the old woman that dispensed coffee in the
market. He did not patronize them, they were to him as good
as the rest, as good as he, only temporarily dimmed and ob-
scured.

"True, he knew, and intimately knew, the better-off and
educated people as well as the poorest and most ignorant. Merchants, lawyers, doctors, scholars, and writers were among his
friends. But the people he knew best and liked most were
neither the rich and conventional, nor the worst and poorest,
but the decent-born middle-life farmers, mechanics, carpenters,

pilots, drivers, masons, printers, deck hands, teamsters, drovers,
and the like. These and their wives and children, their old
fathers and mothers, he knew as no one I think ever knew
them before, and between him and them (especially the old
folks, the mothers and fathers) in numberless instances existed
the warmest attachments.

" He made himself familiar with all kinds of employments,
not by reading trade reports and statistics, but by watching
and stopping hours with the workmen (often his intimate
friends) at their work. He visited the foundries, shops, rolling
mills, slaughter-houses, woollen and cotton factories, shipyards,
wharves, and the big carriage and cabinet shops — went to
clam-bakes, races, auctions, weddings, sailing and bathing parties, christenings, and all kinds of merry-makings."

Wherever the concourse of men was most vivid and
significant, there Whitman betook himself habitually.
When, years later, self-expression came to him, he
wrote often in prose and in verse of the ferries, for
example, and few passages of his work are better
known than these. In those dumb days of which
we speak, however, his attention was doubtless not
sharply focussed on what he saw and heard; the sensations that poured in upon him were being stored up
against the time when complete consciousness of himself should burst open within him, as it were, and all
his rich memories of sights and sounds should take
on meaning. He haunted Broadway also, where the
whole world seemed ceaselessly to pass as in a pageant,
observing it by preference from the top of one of the
old omnibuses. With the drivers of these he was
well acquainted, and he wrote of them subsequently
in a passage which deserves to be quoted here, as
indicative throughout of his love of crowds and of his
passion for companionship: —

"One phase of those days must by no means go unrecorded —namely, the Broadway omnibuses, with their drivers. The vehicles still (I write this paragraph in 1881) give a portion of the character of Broadway — the Fifth avenue, Madison avenue, and Twenty-third street lines yet running. But the flush days of the old Broadway stages, characteristic and copious, are over. The Yellow-birds, the Red-birds, the original Broadway, the Fourth Avenue, the Knickerbocker, and a dozen others of twenty or thirty years ago, are all gone. And the men specially identified with them, and giving vitality and meaning to them — the drivers — a strange, natural, quick-eyed and wondrous race —(not only Rabelais and Cervantes would have gloated upon them, but Homer and Shakspere would) — how well I remember them, and must here give a word about them. How many hours, forenoons and afternoons — how many exhilarating night-times I have had — perhaps June or July, in cooler air — riding the whole length of Broadway, listening to some yarn, (and the most vivid yarns ever spun, and the rarest mimicry) — or perhaps I declaiming some stormy passage from Julius Cæsar or Richard, (you could roar as loudly as you chose in that heavy, dense, uninterrupted street-bass.) Yes, I knew all the drivers then, Broadway Jack, Dressmaker, Balky Bill, George Storms, Old Elephant, his brother Young Elephant (who came afterward,) Tippy, Pop Rice, Big Frank, Yellow Joe, Pete Callahan, Patsy Dee, and dozens more; for there were hundreds. They had immense qualities, largely animal — eating, drinking, women — great personal pride, in their way — perhaps a few slouches here and there, but I should have trusted the general run of them, in their simple good-will and honor, under all circumstances."

As Whitman's love of solitude was associated, moreover, with his enjoyment of classic literature, so his love of companionship was linked with the love of those forms of art which are addressed to men in groups or masses — oratory, the drama, the opera. In many passages of his verse and of his reminiscences he refers to the deep impression made upon him by

these means. New York was rich in opportunities,
and, during this period and later, he often heard the
greatest orators and the greatest singers of his time.
He was frequent in his attendance at the theatre and
the opera, and he records that his excellent habit was
to read beforehand, if he could, the text of the play,
and to revolve in his own mind the playwright's words,
in this way enriching his appreciation of the artist's
impersonation.

Thus stimulated by meditation in lonely places, by
classic literature, by companionship with his fellows of
every sort, by great acting and fine music, Whitman's
emotional life, we may surmise, grew yearly more rich
and full.   His powers of expression meanwhile, as we
shall now see, lagged far behind his keenness of sensa-
tion and perception.

Whitman's short stories, of which for the convenience of bibliographers I subjoin a list,[1] belong

---

[1] 1. Death in the School Room, *Democratic Review*, August,
1841 ; 2. Wild Frank's Return, same, November,1841 ; 3. Ber-
vance : or Father and Son, same, December, 1841; 4. Tomb
Blossoms, same, January, 1842 ; 5. The Last of the Sacred
Army, same, March, 1842 ; 6. The Child Ghost, or the Tale of
the Last Royalist, same, March, 1842 ; 7. A Legend of Life and
Love, same, July, 1842 ; 8. The Angel of Tears, same, September, 1842 ; 9. Eris: a Spirit Record, *Columbian*, March, 1844 ;
10. Dumb Kate : Story of an Early Death, same, May, 1844 ;
11. The Little Sleighers, same, September, 1844 ; 12. The Child
and the Profligate, same, October, 1844 ; 13. The Death of
Windfoot, *American Review*, May, 1845 ; 14. The Boy Lover,
same, June, 1845 ; 15. Revenge and Requital : Tale of a Mur-
derer Escaped, *Democratic Review*, July and August, 1845 ;
16. A Dialogue [against capital punishment], same, November, 1845 ; 17. Little Jane, Brooklyn *Eagle*, December 7, 1846,

mainly to the first part of the decade. About half of
them appeared in the *Democratic Review*, then the
foremost literary publication in the United States, to
which the more important contemporary writers were
also contributing. These little attempts at fiction do
not differ greatly from the current work of the same
period. In general they aim to seize upon the more
unusual and tragic elements in real life, particularly
those that illustrate some moral principle, and to
heighten them into melodrama. A brutal schoolmas-
ter beats a boy who seems asleep at his desk, but who
has suddenly died from heart disease; a young man on
a sudden impulse kills one who has defrauded him of
his money; a wild lad is dragged to death by his own
horse; a sensitive youth pines away with grief at the
death of the girl he loves; a profligate is redeemed by
his protecting affection for a child; a cruel father
shuts his son in a madhouse, — these are all incidents
which may in their essence have come to his attention
first as facts, and were then put into the melodramatic
narrative form then fashionable in America. In substance, the sketches show a sensitive mind, an affectionate nature, a sympathy for suffering humanity. In form,
they are scarcely praiseworthy : the characters are gro-
tesque, the plot is invariably far too rapid for clear
development. They belong to the days when American
writers were still fumbling with the short story, and
only Poe and Hawthorne had shown any skill. In

probably reprinted from elsewhere ; 18. Lingave's Temptation.
Numbers 1, 2, 6, 10, 12, 14, 15 (in part under the title of
One Wicked Impulse), 17, and 18 were reprinted in *Prose
Works* (*Pieces in Early Youth*) ; the original place of publica-
tion of 18 is not known.

style, they do not rise above the commonplace, except
in a few passages in which he obviously wrote under
the influence of Poe.

In brief, Whitman's experiments in fiction must
soon have convinced him that he was striving for
expression in a form unfriendly to his genius, which
lay in his extraordinary power to depict, in rhythmical language, and with kaleidoscopic rapidity, the
multiplicity of detail in life, always emphasizing meanwhile a common emotional element that connects the
apparently divergent phenomena. His immense acquaintanceship with the facts of life, his passion for
people, individually and in the mass, gave him material which, in another mind, might have been fused
into great fiction; but his temperament closed to him
the doors of this form of art.

The same comments may be made on his more ambi-
tious experiment, a novel called *Franklin Evans, or
the Inebriate,* which was issued November 23, 1842, as
an extra number of the *New World,* having been previously advertised as "by a popular American author,
one of the best novelists in the country." It was a
paper quarto of thirty-four pages, and was sold for
twelve and a half cents a copy, or at the rate of ten
copies for a dollar. Twenty thousand copies were disposed of, and Whitman was the richer by a moderate
sum. The comparatively large circulation of the volume was partly due, perhaps, to the fact that it was
issued in a series where it stood side by side with
reprints of Dickens's *American Notes,* Macaulay's *Bal-
lads,* and novels of Bulwer Lytton, and partly because
it was, as the publishers announced, "written with a
view to aid the great work of reform, and rescue young

men from the demon of intemperance." It was a
loosely written, moral, and highly melodramatic tale,
in which a Long Island lad, be-deviled and besotted
by drink, sinks lower and lower in vice and crime
until at last, his eyes opened by disaster, he signs the
pledge of total abstinence. Whitman himself was
always a temperate man, but by no means a total
abstainer, and the tone of the book is one of sincerity,
though it is plain that his zeal for his art carried the
young writer beyond the limits of his conviction. An
old acquaintance of Whitman's relates that Whitman
had once spoken to him of having refreshed himself,
in the midst of his labours on this tract, with gin cock-
tails, and Whitman in later years scorned the crude
art and sentimentalism of the book, and thought of
himself as having outgrown the barren formalism of
the doctrine which he then enunciated. At the time,
however, he seems to have been no less sincere in
this instance than in his contemporaneous pleas for
other reforms.

The poems[1] known to have been written by Whit-

[1] These are: 1. Each has his Grief, *New World*, supple-
ment, November 20, 1841 ; 2. The Punishment of Pride, same,
December, 1841 ; 3. Ambition, *Brother Jonathan*, January 29,
1842 ; 4. Death of the Nature Lover, same, March, 1843 ;
5. Dough-face Song, New York *Evening Post*, about 1848 ;
6. Blood-money, known to have appeared in the same, 1853,
but said by Whitman to have been first printed in the *Tribune*,
and dated in *Pieces in Early Youth*, April, 1843; 7. Wounded
in the House of Friends, said by Whitman to have appeared in
the *Tribune ;* 8. Sailing the Mississippi at Midnight, New Orleans
Crescent, March 6, 1848. Numbers 5, 6, 7, and 8 are reprinted in
Pieces in Early Youth. The date of number 8, together with other
information relating to Whitman's work on the *Crescent*, has
been kindly furnished me by W. K. Dart, Esq., of New Orleans.

man previous to 1850 are thin, amateurish, moralizing productions, of a kind thoroughly familiar to readers of old American and English periodicals. It is in vain that we search them for hints of his later manner. It is sufficient for the biographer to record their names and the dates at which they appeared, and to pass on without further comment. It is not out of these casual experiments that Whitman's art grew.

His professional writing, finally, as shown in his editorials in the *Eagle*, though somewhat too colloquial and disjointed for genuine power, was simple and unaffected, sound in judgment, familiar in tone, and usually clear in expression. He gossips artlessly about the weather; he exhorts his readers to quit physic and blood-letting, and to bathe with regularity; he describes, pleasantly enough, such sights as seem to him most striking; he interests himself in local reforms, rebukes trades-unions, but champions a living wage. Nor is he lacking in interest in national problems of ethics. He argues shrewdly against capital punishment, urges a kindlier treatment of animals, inveighs against the slave trade, though he realizes that " you can't legislate men into virtue. We wouldn't give a snap for the aid of the legislature in forwarding a purely moral revolution! It must work its way through individual minds. It must spread from its own beauty, and melt into the hearts of men — not to be forced upon them at the point of the sword, or by the stave of the officer." In political matters, though, particularly during his sojourn in New Orleans, he was sometimes tempted to

The discovery of several items in this list, and in the list of prose writings on page 26, is due to the patient investigations carried on by Miss Charlotte Morgan.

despair of the republic, he showed a large hopefulness. For definite political parties he cared little. He found slight difference between the Democratic party — his own — and the opposition. Each had its demagogues and "ignorant, ill-bred, passionate men." But he objected in general to the class, in any modern nation, "who looked upon all men as things to be governed — as having evil ways that cannot be checked better than by law; a class who point to the past and hate innovation." He casts his fortunes, on the contrary, with the class who wish "to deal liberally with humanity, to treat it in confidence, and give it a chance of expanding through the measured freedom of its own nature and impulses." In a brief essay on "Art Singing and Heart Singing," in the *Broadway Journal*, moreover, he showed a like broad-mindedness in advocating the development of a national school of music, which should be a full expression of all the characteristics and idiosyncrasies of the United States — of democracy and Americanism.

In spite of the sound sense and kindly feeling of the writings of this type, however, there is nothing that presages the special beauty of Whitman's prose style. As in fiction and verse, this was for him a decade merely of beginnings, of necessary but unsuccessful experiments in alien forms. In spite of his rapid intellectual and emotional growth, he was still dumb. He was trying to express himself in the words of others, and his own lips had not yet been unsealed.

Up to the very end of this period, then, we find in Whitman only the faintest traces, in habits, in aims, in tone and character of expression, of the greater personality he was so soon to become. Successively com-

positor, teacher, journalist, he had satisfied the main
requirements of each profession without attaining distinction. He was, roughly speaking, still a mediocre
man, to all intents and purposes. He knew the country and the city, the East and the Southwest; he had
an exceptionally large and varied acquaintance. His
dress was conventional, no less than his style as a
writer: in no respect had he broken away from the
current artifices of society. He was in thorough
health, calm and dignified in bearing, and free from
petty vices. He was heartily fond of literature and
music. He meditated much. With less literary training, with fewer literary associations, he had a wider and
deeper knowledge of the life of American citizens, and
a deeper sympathy with them, than any other writer of
his time. But nothing in his dormant, undeveloped
personality served to indicate the extraordinary height-
ening of power which was so soon to make him one of
the most remarkable men of his time. An observant
contemporary, acquainted with all the facts, could have
only said that if genius were to be late born in such a
man; if such a mind and body were to be vitalized by
some unknown, some tremendously dynamic force; if
such a placid mortal were to be transformed into a
poet or prophet, he would at least be unique. It was
not along conventional lines that such a spirit could
be developed.

CHAPTER III

It is still to be hoped that documents of some sort exist which will throw light upon Whitman's life between his return from New Orleans and the first appearance of *Leaves of Grass* in 1855. During these years he wrote much, and yet we have virtually nothing that will indicate the nature of the marvellous change that was taking place in him. He had many friends, but apparently none who cared for literature, or who were sufficiently acute to appreciate the transformation that was being wrought before their eyes. And in his own reminiscences, full as they are, there is little that bears closely upon the matter. At thirty-one he was a somewhat indolent newspaper writer, with an undeveloped style — the sign of a mind that had not yet come to self-knowledge. At thirty-six he had written a series of extraordinary poems, original both in form and in substance. And yet the genesis of this novel form and substance remains practically unknown, — such are the miracles that nature works. But nature does not leap, and we must endeavour as best we can to bridge the gap and understand the change.

Returning from his short trip to the South in 1848, Whitman rejoined his family, then living in Brooklyn. There was the father, and his sons Walt and George and Jeff, all able-bodied men, besides the disabled Edward, the mother, the daughter Hannah and, a little later, Mattie, Jeff's wife. It was a patriarchal household of the old type, the men labouring outside the house, and the women doing the simple domestic tasks without assistance. Into this life Whitman settled himself without delay and without friction. The clan was in comfortable circumstances, and it was merely necessary that he should contribute his share to the living expenses, — a share which he always paid, though sometimes intermittently. At first he had a small bookstore and printing-office, and edited and published the *Freeman*, a weekly free-soil paper, but within a year his part in this venture came to an end. He then associated himself with his father in the mingled trade and business of master-carpenter and builder, erecting small frame houses, which were sold on completion. At that epoch Brooklyn was growing rapidly, such speculation was profitable, and Whitman was soon in the way to become well-to-do, when, early in 1855, at about the time of his father's death, he gave up his work without explanation. His duty to himself lay more heavily on him than did money-making.

Meanwhile his daily habits were simple. He spent the day with his workmen, taking with him his dinner pail, and a book, a magazine, or even an article torn from a magazine, — generally prose, and invariably serious matter, — over which he could ponder during the noon hour. His holidays and the intermissions in his work he spent, in good weather, in the open air, often at the seashore, where he read and bathed and thought and wrote. In the evening he frequently

crossed the ferry to the city, where he visited the
theatre or opera, or walked and meditated, continuing
and increasing his acquaintanceship with all classes of
men, but especially with workingmen, and more particularly with ferry-hands and stage-drivers. The
lesser journalists and other members of the Bohemian
world he met at Pfaff's restaurant, but it was apparently not until after 1855 that he became a frequent
visitor there. It was a life of regular labour and much
meditation, under the constant stimulus of city life,
and without influences from the conventional world
of letters.

Whitman, then, was a workman and, in a modest
way, an employer of labour and a man of business,
but he never dreamed of leaving the ranks. He was
not the workman who strains every nerve to make and
save money, and thus become in his turn a capitalist.
Instead, he made as little as possible. With antique
simplicity, he had, like Thoreau, decreased the de-
nominator of life's fraction, instead of increasing its
numerator. He was unmarried; his dress was simple,
his expenses small; a few dollars a week covered his
share for food in the house of his clan. All his sur-
plus time and energy were going — unknown even to
his closest friend — to the enrichment of his emotional
and intellectual life.

Perhaps too much has been made even of Whitman's
reading, which might be supposed to constitute a
slight bond between him and the world of organized
tradition and learning. It is true that he was familiar
with Shakspere and had read other great authors, but
there is nothing to show that at this critical period of
his life he was steeped in literature, or that literature

was an active influence in his development. Emerson he must have read sufficiently to catch some of the main points of his doctrine and to be somewhat impressed by his style. But, generally speaking, he read for knowledge rather than for inspiration. Perhaps he would instinctively have preferred to learn by the ear, for he was a shrewd questioner and made notes of what he acquired in conversation. In default of first-hand information by word of mouth he turned to serious books and particularly to magazines, taking them apparently by chance, wherever an article seemed to promise instruction. These he read and marked and annotated, sucking the very marrow from the bones. Of organized knowledge, of the systematized learning of the libraries, of that vast structure of classified information that we call scholarship, he had no real conception. He handled books clumsily; he was not a bookman. To him reading was merely an adjunct of the power of observation, an additional and secondary means of accumulating percepts. His mental digestion, however, was perfect. Longfellow, the typical bookman, read incessantly, as the records in his journal show, but read, as it were, merely to exercise his eyes, to keep fresh his linguistic knowledge, and to find hints for the use of his fancy: his comments show little acumen. But among Whitman's papers dating from this period we already begin to find wise and shrewd memoranda on books and authors, foreshadowing his later criticism, which, though fragmentary, is perhaps more consistent, more stimulating, and of more permanent value than that of any of his contemporaries.

Books were not the most potent influence in this

period of preparation through which he was uncon-
sciously passing. His passion was for the outer world,
the tangible world. He preferred to learn directly
from things and through people. He haunted the opera,
the theatre, shows, museums, and collections of all
kinds, listening, comparing, absorbing. The great city,
growing greater by leaps and bounds, and cosmopoli-
tan from the first, he knew as did few others, in all
its nooks and corners, through all its grades of occupation and nationality. In this knowledge he sub-
merged himself utterly and for long periods, as a great
scholar in his sources and authorities, as a great
scientist in the observation of his material. The little
group in the great mass that represented education,
culture, and traditional refinement he did not so
much ignore as put in its position of inferiority : he
craved the knowledge of the whole; he was possessed
by the passion for humanity. A man of the crowd,
he loved Broadway : — and Broadway perhaps most
when, packed with people, it welcomed some great
citizen — " all that indescribable human roar and
magnetism, unlike any other sound in the universe —
the glad, exulting thunder-shouts of countless unloos'd
throats of men." And he was similarly moved, he
tells us, by the concourse at the Old Bowery Theatre : —
"pack'd from ceiling to pit with its audience mainly
of alert, well-dress'd, full-blooded young and middle-
aged men, the best average of American-born mechanics — the emotional nature of the whole mass
arous'd by the power and magnetism of as mighty
mimes as ever trod the stage — the whole crowded
auditorium, and what seeth'd in it, and flush'd from
its faces and eyes, to me as much a part of the show

as any — bursting forth in one of those long-kept-up
tempests of hand-clapping peculiar to the Bowery —
no dainty kid-glove business, but electric force and
muscle from perhaps 2000 full-sinew'd men." Such
was the real course of education through which Whitman passed. In his craving for knowledge of things
human he was packing his mind with almost limitless
acquisition of material, — material not so much analyzed and classified as absorbed, until the very mass
of it brought steadily nearer the time when expression
was necessary and inevitable.

In outward appearance, Whitman came back from
the South "looking older and wiser," to use the words
of his brother George. His hair and beard were
tinged with gray. About this time, too, he changed
his manner of dress. Hitherto he had retained the
garb of the journalist, attaching himself thus to what
we vaguely call the upper classes. Now he chose to
wear the more becoming and more appropriate dress
of the workman, and the familiar daguerreotype of
1854, used in the first edition of the *Leaves of Grass*,
represents him as such, in shirt and trousers, with one
hand on his hip and the other in his pocket, a soft
black hat on his head. The relaxed pose is that of
the labourer off duty, and, perhaps on account of the
small size of the daguerreotype, which throws the
emphasis on the body rather than the face, one gets
an impression of aggressive masculinity; but the face
itself, when examined closely, is earnest and solemn,
even wistful. More impressive still is another daguerreotype of the same year, in which only the head and
shoulders appear. The garb is the same, but the
head is uncovered, and the features are more distinct.

The hair is not long, the grayish beard is well trimmed, and these frame in a face of wonderful power and beauty — large features, a full mouth slightly opened as if in speech, a large nose, quiet, penetrating eyes, and the peculiar look of the mystic, the man who sees beyond outward phenomena into the world beyond. In the next decade his face seemed shorter and chubbier and his dress was less becoming. It was only in later life that he regained this air of the poet and the prophet.

His personal characteristics at the time are best indicated in the reminiscences of his brother George, which have special reference to this period. Whitman was cool, " never flurried, curiously deliberate in all his actions "; reticent to the point of stubborn reserve, gentle and conciliating in intercourse with others, plain in his way of living, and abstemious in his food. Alcoholic drinks he used only rarely, and he did not smoke. He was clean and chaste in speech and conduct, and was not known even to pay attention to women. He went his own way, never asking counsel of others. He did not " seem greater than others — just different."

The first distinguishing element of the new writings of Whitman, when they at last appeared, emerging, as it were, from the depths of his solitary broodings, was their form ; and it is simplest to begin our account of his real work with this thread in hand. His chosen medium was an unrhymed species of free verse, — at first recognizable as verse only because it was printed as such, — without an obvious metrical pattern, but containing at intervals brief phrases or passages which the attention at once seized as regularly iambic or dactylic. It has often been compared with the rhythm of

Ruskin, or other so-called prose-poets, in their highest flights, and condemned as being merely balanced prose arranged in the printed form of verse. Yet to many ears Whitman's rhythm is finely musical, and one ends by finding behind its apparent vagaries a norm, habitual or typical, to which it is constantly approximating, but which nevertheless has not yet been formulated. Professor Scott, who has made the most careful study of this rhythm, speaks of Whitman's "delicate susceptibility to certain modes of motion and sequences of sound, particularly the free swaying, urging motions of the ferry-boat, the railroad train, the flight of the birds, and, among sounds, those of the wind, the locusts in the treetops, and the sea." Whitman himself was accustomed to speak of his lines as seemingly "lawless at first perusal, although on closer examination a certain regularity appears, like the recurrence of lesser and larger waves on the sea-shore, rolling in without intermission and fitfully rising and falling." It is plain, in brief, that he had conceived of a delicate but definite rhythmical form or verse-tune, which he always kept in mind, and to which he wrote, approaching it by many corrections, which it is easy to see from his successive drafts that he often made for the sake of the form as distinguished from that of the sense.

There has been much debate — futile because wholly rhetorical — as to whether this rhythmical form, lying on the border of the two provinces, shall be called prose or poetry. It is both and neither, and the common-sense of the matter seems to be that we lack an unambiguous term to describe it, the traditional nomenclature of art being faulty in this respect as in others. Let us be content, however, here to call it

verse, meaning thereby to describe its more predomi-
nant element and to indicate its high value in the scale
of emotional expression.

We shall be wise, then, if without discussing the
name of this new art form, we look at its origin.
Plainly it is not a development from Whitman's early
verse or his early prose, nor is it a combination of both.
His known poetical productions, as late as 1849, were
crude in form, but conventional. *Blood Money* and
In the House of his Friends are plainly transitional
forms, but their dates are still uncertain. His usual
prose, down to as late as 1864, as shown in a published
letter to the mayor and common council of Brooklyn,
is straightforward but stiff, without signs of developing along rhythmical lines. Unless, therefore, some
missing link can be found, we can safely conclude that
the new form came about in a new way, without special
reference to his earlier habits of composition.

It seems clear also that Whitman did not light on
his characteristic form of expression by imitation.
With Blake's experiments he was not familiar. The
balanced verse of the Bible, our common heritage, was
undoubtedly an element in his invention, but it was
plainly not a predominating or essential element.
The Ossianic formula, faintly akin, he knew, but he
recognized it as alien to his spirit, and he jotted down
among his many memoranda at this period the command unto himself that he was, at all costs, not to fall
into that method. Tupper's verse was familiar to him,
and has some similarity to that which he adopted,
though more in matter than in rhythm, but it would
be absurd to find in Tupper's flat and unmelodious
style more than a bungling reaction against conven-

tional forms.   Emerson and others of his school had
long sighed for a new poetic medium, and had from
time to time made divers experiments, but neither the
vague theory nor the uncertain practice could have
aided Whitman.   The suggestion of a prototype in
Samuel Warren's *The Lily and the Bee* seems at first
to offer a fair parallel ; but careful comparison reveals
the distinct difference of key and tone between the
two methods, and makes it improbable that either
could have served as a model for the other.   Moreover,
The Lily and the Bee was not published in England
until 1851, and by March 31, 1851, Whitman had
already found the key to his new style, for in a lecture
delivered on that day before the Brooklyn Art Union
occur characteristic verses that afterwards found a
natural place in one of his longer poems.

The passage in this lecture seems to me to give the
clew.   Whitman's verse-method grew of his own impassioned speech.   As long as he wrote for the eye
only, he followed the conventional forms of literature,
both in prose and in verse, without showing unusual
ability.   It was only when he began to conceive himself as speaking that he found himself following un-
certainly a faint, new, and inner rhythm, as it were
that of his own pulses : —

" Talk not so much, then, young artist, of the great old
masters who but painted and chiselled.   Study not only their
productions.   There is a still better, higher school for him who
would kindle his fire with coal from the altar of the loftiest and
purest art.   It is the school of all grand actions and grand virtues, of heroism, of the deaths of captives and martyrs — of all
the mighty deeds written in the pages of history — deeds of
daring and enthusiasm and devotion and fortitude.   Read well
the death of Socrates.   Read how slaves have battled against

their oppressors — how the bullets of tyrants have, since the
first king ruled, never been able to put down the unquenchable
thirst of man for his rights.

" In the sunny peninsula where art was transplanted from
Greece and generations afterward flourished into new life, we
even now see the growth that is to be expected among a people
pervaded by a love and appreciation of beauty. In Naples, in
Rome, in Venice, that ardor for liberty which is a constituent
part of all well-developed artists and without which a man
cannot be such, has had a struggle — a hot and baffled one.
The inexplicable destinies have shaped it so. The dead lie
in their graves ; but their august and beautiful enthusiasm is
not dead : —

> " Those corpses of young men,
> Those martyrs that hung from the gibbets,
> Those hearts pierced by the gray lead,
> Cold and motionless as they seem
> Live elsewhere with undying vitality ;
> They live in other young men, O kings,
> They live in brothers again ready to defy you.
> They were purified by death ;
> They were taught and exalted.
> Not a grave of those slaughtered ones
> But is growing its seed of freedom,
> In its turn to bear seed,
> Which the wind shall carry afar and re-sow,
> And the rain nourish.
> Not a disembodied spirit
> Can the weapons of tyrants let loose
> But it shall stalk invisibly over the earth
> Whispering, counselling, cautioning."

The style of Whitman's discourse is strikingly like
that of Emerson, with whose essays or lectures we
must probably assume him to be familiar. This prose
style of address, unlike his prose style when he was
writing only for others to read, tended to flower into

a form of free verse that has a strong resemblance to
the verse of the *Leaves of Grass*. I venture to guess
that it was in some such way that Whitman discovered the only medium which would serve him in his
desire for self-expression, for a form of expression that
would parallel his peculiar emotional states, and would
tend to produce in others emotional states of the same
kind.

What psychology has to tell us about the whole
language process may lend some weight to the con-
jecture. The poet's words are but the crude and outward symbols of that inner language, that subtle play
of mental imagery, that unusual and individual combination of percepts which is his real distinction. His
words are only the accompaniment of his thought:
they come to him in various ways, according to the
predominance in him — habitual or momentary — of
one part or another of the somewhat intricate psychological mechanism by which alone may words spring
up within our consciousness in alliance with our
thought. We have, it would appear, a storehouse of
memories of words seen, from which certain visual
images, apparitions — as it were — detach themselves
automatically at our need; and corresponding, but separate, storehouses of words heard, and spoken, and
written. On these four treasuries, heaped up by the
action of the eye and the ear and the muscles of the
throat and hand, all language ultimately depends.
Now the lettered poet may find his medium without
difficulty, because his eye-treasury is highly developed
by much reading, or because his hand-treasury is so
full that words come easily when he takes up his pen.
But Whitman was unlettered and came of an unlet-

tered race; such treasuries in his brain gave him only
normal aid and stimulus. As long as he depended
upon them, he followed merely the dull conventions
of literature, and his expression lagged behind his
thought. The incredible activity and richness of his
inner life only reached expression — such is my hypothesis — when he began to make use of the treasure-
houses of the heard and the spoken word — those most
ancient of language associations in the history of the
race. When he trusted to his ear and his voice, when
he spoke aloud or to himself, the floodgates swung
open. To the great mass of intricately allied inner
phenomena of his mind was added a characteristic and
individual form of expression.

Whether one gives credence or not to such a theory,
however, the fact remains that at the period at which
Whitman found his new style, he was possessed with
the idea of communicating his ideas to others through
the medium of public discourse. He wrote "barrels"
of lectures, his brother George recalled, which still
exist in the shape of a multitude of notes, outlines,
and short passages, some of which have been published
by his executors. They were written either at this
time or a little later, when, with the comparative failure of *Leaves of Grass* to reach the public, his old
faith in his power to thrill mankind by the music of
the spoken word blazed up again in full force. The
new form hovered between prose and verse; it was
living, musical, rhythmical, impassioned speech. If
it had a prototype or an origin, it may be said to have
been born of the rhythm which he heard in nature
and of his memories of the arias and recitatives of
the Italian opera.

Whitman was, then, impelled to speak unto the
sons of men, and after much search he found a new
way, his own special rhythm and music. What message was he to utter ?

If Whitman had been constituted as other men,
susceptible as they to conventional rhythm, he would
have written in metre and rhythm. But he was not
so constituted. Similarly, if he had the conventional
education, and the associations with his fellow-men,
common to other men of letters, he would perhaps
like them have used the ordinary poetic material.
But he had both a new poetic medium and new poetic
matter. He drew his inspiration from another world,
a world circumambient about his contemporaries but
one whose existence they ignored or were ignorant of.
Ours is the world of the minority — that of the stable
folk of education and recognized position. At this
period Whitman knew this world only slightly, and
he never knew it well; his real sympathies and affilia-
tions were with the vast world of artisans and labourers.
In New England there was perhaps a time when ele-
mentary education was so widespread, and literary
and religious influences so pervasive, that these worlds
tended to overlap and merge; and under such conditions Whittier was born and lived, in full sympathy
with a special and local class of somewhat sophisticated workmen. But in the Middle States, and particularly in the great city, the situation then and now
was widely different. Separate oneself by a hand's
breadth, as it were, from the world to whom books
are even partly familiar, and one reaches the multitude of those who live and toil and love and hate
outside the faintest influences of literature and art

and philosophy. They read, perhaps, but only scraps from the newspapers. They are unconscious of the past and unmindful of the future. Science and learning and art are mere words to them. They take life as it is, and have few theories about it. Between the two worlds is fixed a great abyss.

This world of the majority, on which ours is only tangential, and of which we are so ignorant, and particularly the world of the city labourer, Whitman knew well, and he was the only American man of letters who was thoroughly familiar with it. To Longfellow and Lowell and Holmes it was *terra incognita*, for they had travelled little in their own country, and at home had never passed the social boundaries of their class. Emerson had travelled much, but always as a philosopher, to a large degree unconscious of and unsympathetic with the life of the masses. Whittier alone had something of the same sympathy with the people of the under or basic world, though it was not well developed. He knew the New England country folk, but mainly as the country-bred journalist and politician would know them; he would have dragged them after him into the upper world of enlightenment; he could not have conceived of abandoning himself completely to their illiteracy, to their crude religious feeling, or entire lack of it, to their preoccupation with the physical toil and physical joy of life.

But Whitman was a genuine democrat. America was the great democracy, the land of the great mass. With titanic optimism he believed that the hope of humanity lay in these uneducated, illiterate hordes. Here dwelt inexhaustible energy; here the great vital

force of humanity was blindly forcing onwards. Here
there was no distinction of rank or race, all was equality; here chiefly, rather than in the world of the
minority, was Nature working out her great and mysterious plans. It was the dream of Rousseau and the
French Revolution, of Jefferson and Jackson and of
Lincoln, — an ideal perhaps doomed to be shattered,
but held by Whitman in its fullest and purest form.
It was this America that he was to set forth in his
poems : —

"After years of those aims and pursuits, I found myself remaining possess'd, at the age of thirty-one to thirty-three, with
a special desire and conviction. Or rather, to be quite exact,
a desire that had been flitting through my previous life, or
hovering on the flanks, mostly indefinite hitherto, had steadily ad-
vanced to the front, defined itself, and finally dominated everything else. This was a feeling or ambition to articulate and
faithfully express in literary or poetic form, and uncompromis-
ingly, my own physical, emotional, moral, intellectual, and
æsthetic Personality, in the midst of, and tallying, the momentous spirit and facts of its immediate days, and of current
America — and to exploit that Personality, identified with
place and date, in a far more candid and comprehensive sense
than any hitherto poem or book."

In brief, here was the rarest phenomenon in all
modern literature. Other artisans, and sons of artisans, had reached self-expression, but only on step-
ping-stones of their dead selves, by forfeiting their
birthright, by transforming themselves into members
of the few. But here was one of the many, who had
found not only self-expression but a new medium of
expression; who became articulate without surrender-
ing his personality and his membership in his class.
And, most fortunate of all for humanity, this indi-

vidual chanced to be he whose whole education had
lain in his love of the many, in long association with
them and study of them. That very man of the
people who knew most of the people had found his
tongue, and was determined to speak of what life
meant to him as an embodiment of the many, without
reference to what had been written by the few. For
the first time in our modern centuries a poet had been
born of the people who was not a renegade. Demos
had found its voice.

Whitman's special quality is not sufficiently differentiated from that of his brother poets, however, by
either or both of the preceding considerations. If the
new form and the new matter alone were the active
forces, the resultant would have been far different—
perhaps more serviceable to humanity, perhaps less,
but certainly different. We can, for example, conceive of a less ascetic Whittier, or a Ruskin without
his mediævalism, as finding a new rhythm and applying it to the poetry of democracy. In either case we
should have had a clearer, more easily intelligible
verse, conveying more definite ideas. Whitman's
crowning characteristic was that his poetry of democracy sprang, not from well-defined intellectual con-
cepts, but from an extraordinary mood, from an
intense and peculiar emotion.

Recent progress in psychology and medicine has
prepared us for a closer understanding of those unusual individuals whom we call mystics or saints or
seers or prophets. It matters little whether we regard such men as wise or foolish, as false prophets or
true: their psychological history is much the same.

E

The minds of certain men are so constructed that they
may at times seem to pass beyond themselves and the
pressing actualities of life into a state of ecstatic contemplation, in which the whole universe is apparently
revealed to their eyes under a new and glorious aspect,
in the light of which they thereafter live and act.
Such men are usually neurotic or hysterical, and
attempts have recently been made to find in Whitman
the signs of actual degeneracy, but only in the spirit
of controversy and without any basis in fact. Whitman's family history, however, shows certain ab-
normalities: his eldest brother died insane, his
youngest brother was an imbecile; and it may be that
he inherited an abnormal or perhaps rather super-
normal nervous and emotional activity. One or two
anecdotes of intense susceptibility to fright in his
boyhood, his mother's remark that he was a very
strange child, his own that his early life was singularly unhappy, and the strange revelation of his
childish emotion contained in the poem *Out of the
Cradle endlessly Rocking*, may perhaps help to sub-
stantiate such an hypothesis. At all events we have
the plain fact before us that on no other basis can his
poetic method be fully explained than by regarding it
as in large part the product of that extraordinary
mental condition which we associate with the mystic.

That Whitman must be considered as a mystic
becomes immediately apparent when one examines the
writings of mystics — Oriental or Occidental, mediæval or modern. All show the characteristics which
Professor William James has formulated so precisely.
The mystic has the sense of special knowledge. In
his mood, in his vision, he sees — he knows not how —

the greater scheme of creation and his own relation to
it; but this knowledge is ineffable: it cannot be
uttered; it may only be adumbrated or symbolized.
It is, moreover, a knowledge that brings peace and
joy. The light breaks in upon and pervades the
mystic. The whole universe opens before him. He
sees all and is all. There is no beginning or end
to what he sees; cause and effect are identical; the
spirit of the universe is one, and that spirit is love.
Dr. Bucke, Whitman's first biographer, a physician
and alienist of some repute, and the first to see that
Whitman, scientifically speaking, belongs to this class,
calls this state of feeling cosmic consciousness, and
declares that few of our race and time have entered
into it, but that it is the highest step in the same slow
evolution that ripened the impersonal consciousness of
the animal into the self-conscious spirit of man. So
huge a generalization may well stagger the cautious
critic, but it serves to indicate the nature and extent
of the mystic's experience.

Mystic experience is more familiar in the Orient
than in the Occident and is most often produced by
long and solitary meditation, in which the attention is
intently fixed on a single object until the sense of self-
hood broadens enormously and the spirit seems suddenly to cross the threshold of nature, and the finite
self to rejoin the soul of the universe. But a little
investigation shows it to be more common among
men of letters in recent years than would be at first
imagined. Lowell had ecstatic experiences in which
he received revelations; Symonds was subject to
recurrences of an extreme state of mystical consciousness; and Tennyson passed at times into a sort of

waking trance. "This," he said, "has come upon me
through repeating my own name to myself silently,
till all at once, as it were out of the intensity of the
consciousness of individuality, individuality itself
seemed to dissolve and fade away into boundless
being, and this not a confused state but the clearest,
the surest of the surest, utterly beyond words." And
again, "By God Almighty! there is no delusion in the
matter! It is no nebulous ecstasy, but a state of tran-
scendent wonder associated with absolute clearness of
mind."

Dr. Bucke thinks that he can in the *Leaves of Grass*
identify the traces of Whitman's first remarkable
mystic experience in the passage: —

"I believe in you, my soul, the other I am must not abase itself
        to you,
And you must not be abased to the other.
Loaf with me on the grass, loose the stop from your throat,
Not words, not music or rhyme I want, not custom or lecture,
        not even the best,
Only the lull I like, the hum of your valvèd voice.
I mind how once we lay such a transparent summer morning,
How you settled your head athwart my hips and gently
        turned over upon me,
And parted the shirt from my bosom-bone, and plunged your
        tongue to my bare-stript heart,
And reach'd till you felt my beard, and reach'd till you held
        my feet.
Swiftly arose and spread around me the peace and knowledge
        that pass all the argument of the earth,
And I know that the hand of God is the promise of my own,
And I know that the spirit of God is the brother of my own,
And that all the men ever born are also my brothers, and the
        women my sisters and lovers,
And that a kelson of the creation is love,

And limitless are leaves stiff or drooping in the fields,
And brown ants in the little wells beneath them,
And mossy scabs of the worm fence, heap'd stones, elder,
    mullein and poke-weed.''

In other passages of his verse, and not infrequently
in his prose articles and memoranda, Whitman ex-
presses what Professor James calls his "chronic
mystical perception." "There is," he wrote in later
years, "apart from mere intellect, in the make-up of
every superior human identity, (in its moral completeness, considered as *ensemble*, not for that moral alone,
but for the whole being, including physique,) a wondrous something that realizes without argument, frequently without what is called education (though I
think it the goal and apex of all education deserving
the name) — an intuition of the absolute balance, in
time and space, of the whole of this multifarious, mad
chaos of fraud, frivolity, hoggishness — this revel of
fools, and incredible make-believe and general unset-
tledness, we call *the world;* a soul-sight of that divine
clue and unseen thread which holds the whole con-
geries of things, all history and time, and all events,
however trivial, however momentous, like a leash'd
dog in the hand of the hunter."
We find also frequent records of the more acute
phases of the mystical state : —

"The thought of identity . . . Miracle of miracles, beyond
statement, most spiritual and vaguest of earth's dreams, yet
hardest basic fact, and only entrance to all facts. In such
devout hours, in the midst of the significant wonders of heaven
and earth (significant only because of the *Me* in the centre),
creeds, conventions, fall away and become of no account before
this simple idea. Under the luminousness of real vision, it

alone takes possession, takes value. Like the shadowy dwarf
in the fable, once liberated and looked upon, it expands over
the whole Earth and spreads to the roof of heaven.''

" Lo ! Nature (the only complete, actual poem) existing
calmly in the divine scheme, containing all, content, careless
of the criticisms of a day, or these endless and wordy chatter-
ers. And lo ! to the consciousness of the soul, the permanent
identity, the thought, the something, before [which] the magni-
tude even of Democracy, art, literature, etc., dwindles, becomes
partial, measurable — something that fully satisfies (which those
do not). That something is the *All* and the idea of *All*, with
the accompanying idea of eternity, and of itself, the soul, buoyant, indestructible, sailing Space forever, visiting every region,
as a ship the sea. And again lo ! the pulsations in all matter,
all spirit, throbbing forever — the eternal beats, eternal systole
and diastole of life in things — wherefrom I feel and know that
death is not the ending, as was thought, but rather the real
beginning — and that nothing ever is or can be lost, nor ever
die, nor soul, nor matter.''

The Oriental mystics have defined the various steps
by which, in increasing gradations of self-hypnotiza-
tion, they reach the mood they deliberately seek ; and
modern physiological psychology has accounted for
the phenomenon, and shown how " the vanishing of
the sense of self, and the feeling of immediate unity
with the object, is due to the disappearance, in these
rapturous experiences, of the motor adjustments which
habitually mediate between the constant background
of consciousness (which is the Self) and the object in
the foreground, whatever it may be." If one may
hazard an hypothesis drawn from many details in
Whitman's verse and fragmentary notes, we may
suppose that in his case the mystic experience did
not come, as with Tennyson, entirely from a complete
absorption in self, brought about by the prolonged

reiteration of a word. The habit of muscular repose,
the complete motor quiescence which was so characteristic of him from his boyhood up, afforded the
physical basis. In this state of rapt contemplation
the mind, rather drawn out of itself than concen-
trated within itself, dwelt in rapid succession upon
a multitude of outward objects, until, under this swift
and dionysiac sequence of parallel, unrelated percepts,
there followed the mystic experience, the illusion or
the verity, of knowledge of the Whole. The most
marked characteristic of Whitman's poetic method,
that by which he catalogues or inventories objects,
without close subordination or orderly classification,
is perhaps but the same process on a smaller scale.
The reader's attention reels under the weight of unrelated particulars until, just as the mind refuses to go
further in the hopeless task of coördination, it is suddenly suffused, as it were, with a glow of comprehension, and there is born an impression of totality.

We may feel sure, then, that Whitman was a mystic, and that he discovered, in those months and years
of meditation that preceded the appearance of the
Leaves of Grass, his own means of freeing himself
from the outward and understandable world and of
precipitating himself into the mood of ecstasy. Its
characteristics were two. First, the universe appeared
one: all things revealed themselves to him simultane-
ously, as it were, and on the same plane, as if space
and time had been annihilated. Second, the law of
this world was love. Rank and order vanished; the
lowest and the highest were equal; all were to be
comprehended only by affection. In the light of this
ecstasy, now brightening, now growing dim, he was

to walk for the remainder of his days; henceforward he was the poet of the vision, — the vision of the world as love.

It was early in 1855 that Whitman laid down his tools and devoted himself exclusively to his book. Five times had it been written and rewritten, and he even began to set it up with his own hands, in a little printing shop in Brooklyn. In July it appeared. It was a tall, thin quarto of some ninety broad pages, bound in green cloth, ornamented with flowers. The copyright was secured by Walt Whitman, but the title-page did not bear his name, and no publishing house was indicated. It was advertised as for sale at Fowler & Wells' Phrenological Depot in New York and at a Brooklyn bookstore. The price was at first two dollars, afterwards one dollar. Opposite the title-page was a steel engraving of the now familiar daguerreotype representing Whitman as a workingman.

The preface, ten pages long in double columns, was a rhapsody on the poet's function in America. In form it was scarcely to be distinguished from the less rhythmical parts of his verse, and in a later edition he drew freely from it while composing *On Blue Ontario's Shores*. It was not at all intelligible to the ordinary reader, and that fact doubtless added to the perplexity with which people naturally regarded the novel poems that followed.

These were twelve in number and bore no titles.[1]

[1] Later they were called : Song of Myself ; A Song for Occupations ; To Think of Time; The Sleepers ; I Sing the Body Electric ; Faces; Song of the Answerer ; Europe ; A Boston Ballad; A Child Went Forth; Who Learns my Lesson; Great are the Myths.

The first was the long *Poem of Walt Whitman, an American,* as it was called in the second edition, or *The Song of Myself,* as it was later entitled. Hard to follow at first and in spots virtually unintelligible, it becomes clear when one directs his attention to the general movement of the thought.

The author is but a type, so runs the theory; what he says of himself he says of mankind. His theme is the mood of ecstasy and understanding, which he reaches through the contemplation of nature. Would you have the secret? You may, if you will; but you must seize it instantaneously, as a whole, not derive it by logical steps. The secret is that man and the world are good, are clean and holy, are to be accepted with joy and trustfully. Separate your contemplative self, as I do, from your active, ordinary self: thus will illumination come to you. Let grass be the subject of your thought. What is it? What does it mean? One might quaintly guess it to be a part of God's vesture, — his handkerchief, designedly dropped to provoke curiosity, and "bearing the owner's name some way in the corners"; or as a symbol of Nature's uniformity, her equal proffer to all men; or as the symbol of all that has gone before us — "the beautiful uncut hair of graves." But it is most typical of the ceaselessly evolving universe, working out its gigantic law of transmutation.

That law is love. The universe means well by us. I am a better type than the insentient grass, — I, the momentary symbol of conscious humanity, for I see and am all forms of that pervasive spirit. And here follows a magnificent catalogue of instances that symbolize the infinitude of human experience, including even the beasts, none of whom are unworthy: —

"I do not call the tortoise unworthy because she is not something else ;
And the jay in the woods never studied the gamut, yet trills pretty well to me ;
And the look of the bay mare shames silliness out of me.''

Man, then, — actual, existing man, — "hankering, gross, mystical, nude," is the great type, the great reality. Man is deathless, august; he is himself of the very essence of being. He must then venerate himself, rather than the gods. It follows, then, that virtue and vice are, *sub specie eternitatis,* foolish words. Each plays its part in Nature's dualism: —

" What blurt is this about virtue and about vice ?
Evil propels me, and reform of evil propels me, I stand indifferent.''

The universe holds its steady progress: shall man fear the outcome or dare to distinguish between God's instruments ?

" Did you fear some scrofula out of the unflagging pregnancy?
Did you guess the celestial laws are yet to be work'd over and rectified ? ''

Similarly, in man there can be no degradation or distinction : —

"I speak the pass-word primeval, I give the sign of democracy ;
By God ! I will accept nothing which all cannot have their counterpart of on the same terms.''

And as man is divine only as a perennial element in Nature, he is divine by virtue of his power of self-continuation, by virtue, that is, of his power of propagation. Hence, man's function of propagation and its instruments are, from that point of view, essential and noble.

Again he rushes into tumultuous inventory of multitudinous aspects and instances of life, contemplating with ecstasy all the works of Nature, heroes and martyrs of all ages, man in his most ordinary or most picturesque occupations, even plants and beasts, — the running blackberry vine that " would adorn the parlors of heaven "; the animals that are " so placid and self-contained " : —

" They do not sweat and whine about their condition,
    They do not lie awake in the dark and weep for their sins,
    They do not make me sick discussing their duty to God,
    Not one is dissatisfied, not one is demented with the mania
        of owning things,
    Not one kneels to another, nor to his kind that lived thousands
        of years ago,
    Not one is respectable or unhappy over the whole earth."

All life, then, he loves, and in a wonderful passage he announces himself, in his typical aspect, as the lover of the earth : —

" I am he that walks with the tender and growing night,
    I call to the earth and sea half-held by the night.

" Press close, bare-bosom'd night ! Press close, magnetic, nour-
        ishing night !
    Night of south winds — night of the large few stars !
    Still, nodding night — mad, naked, summer night.

" Smile, O voluptuous, cool-breath'd earth !
    Earth of the slumbering and liquid trees !
    Earth of departed sunset — earth of the mountains misty-topt !
    Earth of the vitreous pour of the full moon just tinged with
        blue !

Earth of shine and dark mottling the tide of the river !
Earth of the limpid gray of clouds brighter and clearer for my
    sake !
Far-swooping elbow'd earth — rich, apple-blossom'd earth !
Smile, for your lover comes !

" Prodigal, you have given me love — therefore I to you give
    love !
O unspeakable, passionate love ! "

Nay, more. So strongly does he feel this transcending
vitality which is his through his secret, that he would
share it with the weak and fainting spirit : —

" O despairer, here is my neck ;
    By God ! you shall not go down !   Hang your whole weight
        upon me.

" I dilate you with tremendous breath, I buoy you up ;
    Every room of the house do I fill with an arm'd force,
    Lovers of me, bafflers of graves.

" Sleep — I and they keep guard all night ;
    Not doubt, not decease shall dare to lay finger upon you ;
    I have embraced you, and henceforth possess you to myself,
    And when you rise in the morning you will find what I tell
        you is so."

Such in the barest outline is Whitman's famous
doctrine, not without its analogies to the idealism of
his predecessors, particularly Emerson. The succeeding poems reinforced and completed it without adding
new elements; but he kept recurring to a thought that
then obtruded itself continually upon him, that the
strength and weakness of the never-ending chain of
life lay always in the present link. Each generation
must be strong and noble, and this means the strength
and nobility of man's body and woman's body. To

this physical basis of the continuation of the race he comes back again and again with joyful insistence, for men and women are the ultimate realities of life; all governments and all religions, all happiness and all progress, depend upon their union.

About eight hundred copies of the *Leaves of Grass* were printed, a sufficient quantity deposited for sale with dealers in New York, Brooklyn, and Boston, and a considerable number sent out for review and to well-known writers. Commercially, the enterprise was a complete failure. Very few copies were sold, and the great bulk of the edition remained on the author's hands. This is not greatly to be wondered at. The public at large cares little for poetry, and particularly for poetry of a novel kind. Whitman's name was virtually unknown, and any ordinary reader who saw the volume must have been puzzled by the odd form, bewildered by the thought, and quite probably shocked by the apparently materialistic and anti-religious tone. Whitman's own family, unaccustomed to reading, could make nothing of it. "I saw the book," his brother George said in later years, — "I didn't read it at all — didn't think it worth reading — fingered it a little. Mother thought as I did — did not know what to make of it. . . . I remember mother comparing *Hiawatha* [which came out the same year] to Walt's, and the one seemed to us pretty much the same muddle as the other. Mother said that if *Hiawatha* was poetry, perhaps Walt's was."

Whitman could not have been greatly surprised at the indifference shown to his poems by those who were indifferent to all poetry   But he must have been bewildered and disheartened by the indifference and hostility of critics and men of letters. The former, almost with one accord, anathematized the volume and the author. It was "muck" and "obscenity" "full of bombast, egotism, vulgarity, and nonsense"; he was a "lunatic"; he was "as unacquainted with art as a hog is with mathematics"; he "deserved the whip of the public executioner." His brother poets, as a rule, ignored the book, or destroyed it, — as did Whittier, — or returned it to the author. This indifference of the intelligent or expert public was, we may guess, due to much the same causes as that of the illiterate public. To be sure, they were familiar with Whitman's transcendental ideas, as expressed in Emerson or Carlyle; but their familiarity was with mysticism expounded in a more or less logical fashion, not with the mystic's own natural utterance. Their ears, too, were ill attuned to the new form, and they were also repelled by the glorification of the common man, of the very dust at their feet.

A still greater stumbling-block to the poet and reader of poetry at that day were the intensity and particularity of Whitman's reference to sexual relations. American life half a century ago is unanimously declared to have been prudish; but even if it had been as daring as it was timid, it might well have been aghast at the full tone of sensuous exaltation, of phallic frenzy, that sounded throughout these poems, finding expression everywhere in sexual imagery. Thoreau thought that the beasts might have so spoken. From our calmer vantage ground of half a century later we can see that he missed the point. No speaking beasts could have been so teleological; it was rather man speaking boldly of his essential de-

lights because he saw them essential to him and to
the race. The discussion has now grown formal
and academic, and whether these matters are, in the
hands of a great poet, *tacenda*, or whether the intense
and lasting emotional life that clusters around the
congress of man and woman must remain always
unexpressed in art, is a matter of cautious doubt.
One thing is clear, however, that Whitman was never
licentious or obscene; no attentive reader could now
so accuse him. But at that time, and for some years
to come, the issue of propriety was constantly raised.[1]

[1] It is necessary to add that the exuberance of sexual imagery in Whitman's work may quite possibly have been due to
a change in his habits of life. As a young man, all testimony
concurs to show him to have been chaste. His first biographer,
however, Mr. Burroughs, speaking of the period 1840-1855, said
that Whitman " sounded all experiences of life, with all their
passions, pleasures, and abandonments." In 1893, moreover,
Whitman himself, writing to John Addington Symonds, plainly
stated that " my life, young manhood, mid-age, times South,
etc., have been jolly bodily, and doubtless open to criticism.
Tho' unmarried, I have had six children — two are dead — one
living Southern grandchild, fine boy, writes to me occasionally
— circumstances (connected with their fortune and benefit)
have separated me from intimate relations." The later portion
of the passage, taken together with the tone of his verse, seems
to me probably to indicate that, though Whitman may have
been caught in the net of accidental passion, his affections had
centred on one or perhaps two women, with whom he had
relations lasting for a considerable number of years, and whom
he may be regarded as having married in all but the name. In
later life, Whitman was averse to mentioning the subject, even
to his most intimate friends, and no further facts are known.
At one time he intended to make a careful statement with
regard to the matter, to be kept sealed, and to be used by his
representatives, in case of need, for the protection of those dear

On the other hand, there were a few critics sufficiently clear-headed and broad-minded to see the
essential greatness of the book in spite of its peculiarities. In an unsigned notice in the *North American
Review*, Edward Everett Hale recognized " the fresh-
ness, simplicity, and reality of the book," and "the
wonderful sharpness and distinctness " of the author's
imagination, declaring, too, that there is not a word in
the volume " meant to attract readers by its grossness." W. J. Stillman, in the *Crayon*, while denying
to it ideality, concentration, and purpose, bore witness
to the " wonderful vigour of thought and intensity of
purpose." In *Putnam's Monthly* an unknown reviewer
was keen enough to see that in its large aspects this
was nothing but Emerson put into practice, the formal
gospel of the New England school coming fresh from
the lips of the people. " A fireman or omnibus driver,
who had intelligence enough to absorb the speculations
of that school of thought which culminated at Boston
some fifteen or eighteen years ago, and resources of
expression to put them forth again in a form of his
own, with sufficient self-conceit and contempt for public taste to affront all usual propriety of diction, might
have written this gross yet elevated, this superficial
yet profound, this preposterous yet somehow fasci-
nating book." And in England a writer in the *Leader*
wrote the following excellent statement — he is often
wiser who views from afar — of the " staggering "
central principle of the *Leaves of Grass* : —

---

to him; but this was never done. We know (and wish to
know) nothing more than that he had at times been lured by
the pleasures of the flesh, like many a poet before him, and
that he had known the deep and abiding love of woman.

"It seems to resolve itself into an all-attracting egotism —
an eternal presence of the individual soul of Walt Whitman
in all things, yet in such wise that this one soul shall be presented as a type of all human souls whatsoever. He goes forth
into the world, this rough, devil-may-care Yankee ; passionately
identifies himself with all forms of being, sentient or inanimate ;
sympathizes deeply with humanity ; riots with a kind of Bac-
chanal fury in the force and fervour of his own sensations ;
will not have the most vicious or abandoned shut out from
final comfort and reconciliation ; is delighted with Broadway,
New York, and equally in love with the desolate backwoods,
and the long stretch of the uninhabited prairie, where the wild
beasts wallow in the weeds, and the wilder birds start upward
from their nests among the grass ; perceives a divine mystery
wherever his feet conduct, or his thoughts transport him ; and
beholds all things tending toward the central and sovereign
Me."

Best of all, Emerson himself, Whitman's sole master
and exemplar, — so far as he may be said to have had
one at all, — recognized at once the extraordinary
merit of the volume, and promptly wrote him as
follows : —

CONCORD, MASS'TTS, 21 JULY, 1855.

"DEAR SIR, I am not blind to the worth of the wonderful
gift of 'Leaves of Grass.'   I find it the most extraordinary
piece of wit and wisdom that America has yet contributed.   I
am very happy in reading it, as great power makes us happy.
It meets the demand I am always making of what seemed the
sterile and stingy Nature, as if too much handiwork, or too
much lymph in the temperament, were making our Western
wits fat and mean.

"I give you joy of your free and brave thought. I have great
joy in it. I find incomparable things said incomparably well,
as they must be. I find the courage of treatment that so de-
lights us, and which large perception only can inspire.

"I greet you at the beginning of a great career, which yet

F

must have had a long foreground somewhere, for such a start. I rubbed my eyes a little, to see if this sunbeam were no illusion ; but the solid sense of the book is a sober certainty. It has the best merits, namely, of fortifying and encouraging.

" I did not know, until I last night saw the book advertised in a newspaper, that I could trust the name as real and available for a post-office.

" I wish to see my benefactor, and have felt much like striking my tasks and visiting New York to pay you my respects.
                                        " R. W. EMERSON."

Emerson was equally free in expressing himself to others in favour of his new-found poet. To a visitor at Concord he said in the first flush of his enthusiasm, Mr. Burroughs records, that "Americans abroad may now come home : unto us a man is born." A little later, when he saw how blind others were to the promise he saw in Whitman, and how loud were the protests, his faith in his own discernment began to weaken, and he wrote to Carlyle half-heartedly : —

" One book, last summer, came out in New York, a nondescript monster, which yet had terrible eyes and buffalo strength, and was indisputably American — which I thought to send you ; but the book throve so badly with the few to whom I showed it, and wanted good morals so much, that I never did. Yet I believe now again, I shall. It is called ' Leaves of Grass ' — was written and printed by a journeyman printer in Brooklyn, New York, named Walter Whitman ; and after you have looked into it, if you think, as you may, that it is only an auctioneer's inventory of a warehouse, you can light your pipe with it."

In the meantime Whitman had not been willing to leave his precious volume to the uninstructed mercy of the public jury. He was more than a poet, we must remember : he stood for a novel theory of composition, for a new attitude towards literature; he was a fierce propagandist for the rights of the people in letters, and as such he was impatient. To three journals whose columns were open to him, therefore, he contributed anonymous reviews — so characteristically worded that the disguise must have been ineffectual to any one who knew him or his book. In the *American Phrenological Journal* of Fowler and Wells, at that time his agents and soon to become his publishers, he compared the *Leaves* with Tennyson's *Maud*, dwelling bluntly on the striking contrast between the vigour, the self-reliance, and the democratic character of the one, and the listlessness, the *ennui*, the indecision, and the aristocratic quality of the other. In the *United States and Democratic Review*, to which he had in years past been a frequent contributor, he sounded the call for an "athletic and defiant" native literature, of which he was himself a symbol. And in the Brooklyn *Times*, with which he seems at that period to have had some connection, he deliberately sets forth his own merits : —

" To give judgment on real poems, one needs an account of the poet himself. Very devilish to some, and very divine to some, will appear the poet of these new poems, the ' Leaves of Grass'; an attempt as they are, of a naïve, masculine, affectionate, contemplative, sensual, imperious person, to cast into literature not only his own grit and arrogance, but his own flesh and form, undraped, regardless of models, regardless of modesty or law, and ignorant or silently scornful, as at first appears, of all except his own presence and experience, and all outside the fiercely loved land of his birth, and the birth of his parents, and their parents for several generations before him. Politeness this man has none, and regulation he has none. A rude child of the people ! — No imitation — no foreigner — but a growth and idiom of America. No discontented — a careless

slouch, enjoying to-day. No dilettante democrat — a man who
is art-and-part with the commonalty, and with immediate life —
loves the streets — loves the docks — loves the free rasping talk
of men — likes to be called by his given name, and nobody at
all need Mr. him — can laugh with laughers — likes the ungen-
teel ways of laborers — is not prejudiced one mite against the
Irish — talks readily with them — talks readily with niggers —
does not make a stand on being a gentleman, nor on learning or
manners — eats cheap fare, likes the strong flavored coffee of
the coffee-stands in the market, at sunrise — likes a supper of
oysters fresh from the oyster-smack — likes to make one at the
crowded tables among sailors and work-people — would leave a
select soirée of elegant people any time to go with tumultuous
men, roughs, receive their caresses and welcome, listen to their
noise, oaths, smut, fluency, laughter, repartee — and can pre-
serve his presence perfectly among these, and the like of these.
The effects he produces in his poems are no effects of artists
or the arts, but effects of the original eye or arm, or the actual
atmosphere, or tree, or bird. You may feel the unconscious
teaching of a fine brute, but will never feel the artificial teaching of a fine writer or speaker.

" Other poets celebrate great events, personages, romances,
wars, loves, passions, the victories and power of their country,
or some real or imagined incident — and polish their work and
come to conclusions, and satisfy the reader. This poet celebrates natural propensities in himself ; and that is the way he
celebrates all. He comes to no conclusions, and does not
satisfy the reader. He certainly leaves him what the serpent
left the woman and the man, the taste of the Paradisaic tree of
the knowledge of good and evil, never to be erased again."

The candid reader's first impression of these self-
praising notices is one of surprise and perhaps dis-
gust, for by tradition the poet is wrapped up in his
art and careless of its reception by the vulgar throng.
But reflection points to a more tolerant attitude.
Writers have, unfortunately, rarely been as self-contained as we may think. Some of great repute have

done as Whitman did, and many have laboured to influence the notices of their work, regarding favourable
criticism as effective advertising. Log-rolling in literature was certainly not extinct in Whitman's time, nor
was his the only offence, if offence it was. And it must
be added that his journalistic experience and his long
acquaintance with newspapers had not taught him to
regard printed criticism as necessarily impartial in its
origin. He acted, in brief, without finesse of feeling, in the downright, whole-hearted way which was
characteristic of him, as the unconventionalized man,
as one of his " roughs," would have acted.

But such good words as appeared about the book
were lost in the chorus of disapproval, and though
Whitman was joyful over Emerson's letter, the situation was disheartening. He paused to consider his
course. " When the book aroused such a storm of
anger and condemnation everywhere," he confessed in
later years, " I went off to the east end of Long
Island and Peconic Bay. Then came back to New
York with the confirmed resolution, from which I
never afterward wavered, to go on with my poetic
enterprise in my own way and finish it as well as I
could."

In June, 1856, he made his second appearance before the public with an enlarged edition, a sixteenmo
of nearly four hundred pages. Only one of the previous poems was omitted. The others were touched
here and there, always for the better, and twenty
were added.[1]

[1] 1. Unfolded out of the Folds; 2. Salut au Monde ; 3.
Song of the Broadaxe ; 4. By Blue Ontario's Shore ; 5. This
Compost; 6. To You; 7. Crossing Brooklyn Ferry; 8. Song

The edition showed not only greater richness of
poetic power, but a more single purpose. The egoistic
note, which in the first edition had seemed to pre-
dominate, was diminishing. The altruistic theme
came out more clearly. It was plainer that *I* meant,
not Walt Whitman, but *man* — the American workman. The subject was democracy : —

> "Painters have painted their swarming groups, and the centre
>   figure of all ;
> From the head of the centre figure spreading a nimbus of gold-
>   color'd light ;
> But I paint myriads of heads, but paint no head without its
>   nimbus of gold-color'd light ;
> From my hand, from the brain of every man and woman it
>   streams, effulgently flowing forever.''

With this thread held firmly in hand, we are less
likely to be misled by the apparent sensuality of
Unfolded and *A Woman Waits for Me*, which he in-
serted to confirm and complete his previous attitude.
It was no wife or mistress of his, but the women of
America, the women of the world, in whose physical

of the Open Road ; 9. A Woman Waits for Me; 10. A poem a
large part of which is left out of the later editions, but which
is partly preserved in " On the Beach at Night Alone." 11.
Excelsior; 12. Song of Prudence ; 13. A poem which now
makes part of the " Song of the Answerer." 14. Assurances ;
15. To a Foil'd European Revolutionaire; 16. A short poem,
part of which is afterwards incorporated in " As I sat Alone by
Blue Ontario's Shore," and the rest omitted from subsequent
editions. 17. Miracles ; 18. Spontaneous Me ; 19. A poem called
" Poem of the Propositions of Nakedness," afterward called
" Respondez," and printed in every subsequent edition down
to that of 1882–'3, but omitted from that. 20. Song of the
Rolling Earth.

keeping are the babes of mankind.   If women be not
strong, where shall strength come to the race?   If
they be impassive and unworthy, prudish and cold-
blooded, ill-natured and hysterical, what can come of
it but a world of weaklings?   For —

" Unfolded out of the folds of the woman, man comes unfolded,
     and is always to come unfolded ;
  Unfolded only out of the superbest woman of the earth, is to
     come the superbest man of the earth ;
  Unfolded out of the friendliest woman, is to come the friend-
     liest man ;
  Unfolded only out of the perfect body of a woman, can a man
     be form'd of perfect body. . . .
  Unfolded out of the folds of the woman's brain, come all the
     folds of the man's brain, duly obedient ;
  Unfolded out of the justice of the woman, all justice is un-
     folded ;
  Unfolded out of the sympathy of the woman is all sympathy :
  A man is a great thing upon the earth, and through eternity —
     but every jot of the greatness of man is unfolded out of
     women ;
  First the man is shaped in the woman, he can then be shaped
     in himself.''

From this glorification of motherhood and fatherhood as they produce " sons and daughters fit for
These States," we pass to the longer new poems.
The splendid *Salut au Monde* is the first of his
few well-articulated poems, a survey of the whole
world — its sounds, its physical aspect, its rivers and
deserts and seas and watercourses and railroads, its
ancient empires and temples and battlefields, its
uttermost parts, its teeming cities, its diverse popula-
tions ; to the lowest and meanest his love goes out.
It is God's whole universe to which he gives friendly

greeting. The same all-embracing sympathy shines
in *Crossing Brooklyn Ferry,* and in it, in the *Song
of the Broadaxe,*[1] and the *Song of the Open Road,*
we find the concentration and unity that mark the
growth of his artistic power. They lack the dove-
tailing accuracy of logical sequence that we find in the
more intellectual poets, but they have a sweeping emotional sequence of transition from mood to cognate
mood that is equally effective. The *Open Road* is
one of the most haunting of all his compositions.
Starting from the highway, which entices one to push
out boldly and carelessly into unknown districts, he
transfers his symbolism to the open road of thought
and feeling and action, urging his friends tenderly to
throw aside convention and conservatism and enter
heartily upon the journey of life, questing for the unknown : —

"Allons! after the Great Companions! and to belong to them!
    They too are on the road! they are swift and majestic men!
        they are the greatest women. . . .

---

[1] The beautiful opening lines of the *Broadaxe,* which ap-
proach closely to conventional metre and rhyme, show what
a tremendous advance in skill Whitman had made in less than
ten years, and hint what he might have done in verse of a more
orthodox character had his temperament not forced him into
the rhapsodical style of the mystic : —

"Weapon shapely, naked, wan!
    Head from the mother's bowels drawn!
    Wooded flesh and metal bone! limb only one, and lip only
        one!
    Gray-blue leaf by red-heat grown! helve produced from
        a little seed sown!
    Resting the grass amid and upon,
    To be lean'd, and to lean on."

"My call is the call of battle—I nourish active rebellion ;
He going with me must go well arm'd ;
He going with me goes often with spare diet, poverty, angry
      enemies, desertions.

"Allons! the road is before us!
It is safe—I have tried it—my own feet have tried it
      well.

"Allons! be not detain'd!
Let the paper remain on the desk unwritten, and the book
      on the shelf unopen'd!
Let the tools remain in the workshop! let the money remain
      unearn'd!
Let the school stand! mind not the cry of the teacher!
Let the preacher preach in his pulpit! let the lawyer plead in
      the court, and the judge expound the law.

"Mon enfant! I give you my hand!
I give you my love, more precious than money,
I give you myself, before preaching or law;
Will you give me yourself? will you come travel with me ?
Shall we stick by each other as long as we live ?"

On the back of the new volume were stamped in
gold letters a few words from Emerson's letter: "I
greet you at the beginning of a great career. R. W.
Emerson." In an appendix, which consisted mainly
of notices, Emerson's letter of July, 1855, was printed
in full, and with it a letter from Whitman which explained his aims : —

" Other work," he says, " I have set for myself to do, to meet
people and The States face to face, to confront them with an
American rude tongue ; but the work of my life is making
poems. I keep on till I make a hundred, and then several hundred—perhaps a thousand. The way is clear to me. A few
years, and the average annual call for my Poems is ten or
twenty thousand copies—more, quite likely. Why should I
hurry or compromise ? In poems or in speeches I say the word

or two that has got to be said, adhere to the body, step with the countless common footsteps, and remind every man or woman of something.

"Master, I am a man who has perfect faith. Master, we have not come through centuries, caste, heroisms, fables, to halt in this land to-day."

The burden of the letter, however, is plea for a more rigorous and manly literature. He is tired of "this empty dish, gallantry, this tepid wash, this diluted deferential love."

"Strangle the singers who will not sing to you loud and strong. Open the doors of the West. . . . America is to be kept coarse and broad. . . . None believes in These States. . . . Not a man faces round at the rest with a terrible negative voice, refusing at all times to be bought off from his own eye-sight. . . . The churches are one vast lie ; the people do not believe them, and they do not believe themselves. . . . I think there can never be again upon the festive earth more bad-disordered persons deliberately taking seats, as of late in These States, at the heads of the public tables — such corpses' eyes for judges — such a rascal and thief in the Presidency."

And finally : —

"Those shores you found. I say you have led The States there — have led Me there. I say that none has ever done or ever can do, a greater deed for The States, than your deed. Others may line out the lines, build cities, work mines, break up farms; it is yours to have been the original true Captain who put to sea, intuitive, positive, rendering the first report, and more by the mariners of a thousand bays, in each tack of their arriving and departing, many years after you.

"Receive, dear Master, these statements and assurances through me, for all the young men, and for an earnest that we know none before you, but the best following you ; and that we demand to take your name into our keeping, and that we understand what you have indicated, and find the same indicated in ourselves, and that we will stick to it and enlarge upon it through These States."

The comments of the press upon the second edition were even more condemnatory than upon the first, for to the thoughtless reader it was apparently more indecent. The public, however, showed a greater interest, — perhaps, we may suspect, for the same reason. A thousand copies[1] — no small number for a volume of poems — was sold in a short time, and preparations for a larger sale were made through agencies in the principal cities in America and in London, Paris, and Brussels. But the cry of public disapproval grew louder and louder, there were threats of prosecution, and finally Fowler and Wells, who, though its real publishers, had not given it their imprint, withdrew their support, and the book was allowed to go out of print.

In spite of the disfavour of the general public Whitman was beginning to attract the attention of men of larger judgment. Emerson is said to have been displeased at the publicity given to his letter, though this was done at the advice of Charles A. Dana, a friend of both Emerson and Whitman; and Whitman himself was innocent of wrong: "I supposed the letter was meant to be blazoned," he said years later; "I regarded it as

[1] In his letter to Emerson, appended to the second edition, Whitman said that the thousand copies of the first edition were readily sold. This seems to contradict flatly the statement made by Burroughs and borne out by Whitman's allusions to the subject later. Perhaps he was merely translating his hopes into facts, or had in mind negotiations, of which we are ignorant, for disposing of the entire remainder of the first edition.

the charter of an emperor." Whatever annoyance
Emerson may have felt, however, had no effect upon
their personal intercourse. He disapproved of the
publication of poems that touched on sexual relations,
but he had a genuine liking for Whitman and came
several times to see him. And even before the publication of the second edition he had begun to point
out Whitman as a man worth knowing. Thus came
Thoreau, greatly puzzled by the " disagreeable " pieces,
but carried out of himself — " put into a liberal
state of mind," as he expressed it, by Whitman's en-
thusiastic optimism ; Bronson Alcott, who saw less of
Whitman than of his mother, from whom he heard endless praises of her son's goodness and wisdom ; and
Moncure D. Conway, who found him basking in the
blazing sun in a pasture, went bathing with him in the
sea, and accompanied him to the Tombs, witnessing a
striking incident of his influence over the warden in
behalf of an ill-used prisoner. Like others, he was
impressed by Whitman's gentleness, modesty of person, and simplicity of manner, by his essential greatness
and nobility of mind, by the magnetic, almost physical
influence, which he exercised over men. William
Cullen Bryant and Henry Ward Beecher came also,
and Lord Houghton, who shared his supper of roast
apples, as George Whitman relates. At this period,
too, Whitman began to make warm friendships in
families of a higher social status than his own, where
he went almost daily, meeting women of more refinement than he had hitherto known, and winning affection and confidence from all.

To grasp the whole of his life, however, we must
not forget his frequent association with labouring men

of all classes, to be described more particularly later on, and his more or less regular meetings with the so-called "Bohemian" set at Pfaff's, a dingy German basement restaurant on Broadway, where actors and journalists were wont to gather. Of the writers many were out of accord with the prevailing tone of American letters, and there was much in their radical programme, developed under French influence, with which Whitman could sympathize, as he could sympathize with anything that tended to break up routine and conventionalism in poetry. But he was, it would seem, for the most part a quiet onlooker and listener amid the clouds of smoke, sitting placidly over his glass of beer, and "emanating," as Mr. Howells, who first saw him there, said, "an atmosphere of purity and serenity."

In the quiet years that immediately followed Whitman gave himself wholly up to his work, living frugally on such means as he had derived from his business pursuits and the sales of his second edition. His first thought was the completion of the *Leaves of Grass*, and there are extant in his huge collection of manuscript notes a multitude of memoranda for revision and addition. He made lists of different themes and suggestive words, and cautioned himself again and again to avoid "all poetical similes — to be faithful to the perfect likelihoods of nature — healthy, exact, simple, disdaining ornaments."

But there was a time also when he conceived of a new point of attack, or rather reverted to an earlier plan of reaching his fellow-countrymen more directly through the spoken word. He was to prepare a whole series of lectures, explaining and fortifying his theories. These would attract the wandering attention of the public to his poetical work, to which it could be regarded as supplementary. It was apparently with such a purpose in mind that he made the memorandum, in June, 1857 : " The Great Construction of the New Bible. Not to be diverted from the principal object — the main life — the three hundred and sixty-five. — It ought to be ready in 1859." His plan was to make himself the great orator of the day, the man who would tell Americans their faults, and instruct them in the social and political virtues. No great personal gain was to be his; his admission fee was to be fifteen or even ten cents; but he was to be the moulder of public opinion. As Washington freed America from the domination of the English government, so Whitman was to free us from the domination of all foreign ideals. On April 24, 1857, he made the memorandum : —

" *True Vista before.* — The strong thought-impression or conviction that the straight, broad, open, well-marked true vista before, or course of public teacher, ' wander-speaker,' — by powerful words, orations, uttered with copiousness and decision, with all the aid of art, also the natural flowing vocal luxuriance of oratory. That the mightiest rule over America could be thus — as for instance, on occasion, at Washington to be, launching from public room, at the opening of the session of Congress — perhaps launching at the President, leading persons, Congressmen, or Judges of the Supreme Court. That to dart hither or thither, as some great emergency might demand — the greatest champion America ever could know, yet holding no office or emolument whatever, — but first in the esteem of men and women. *Not* to direct eyes or thoughts to any of the usual avenues, as of official appointment, or to get such anyway. To put all those aside for good. But always to keep up living interest in public questions — and *always to hold the ear of the people.*"

One of these lectures has been preserved for us, in a rough outline, in *An American Primer*, — "a primer of words for American young men and women, for literats, orators, teachers, musicians, judges, presidents, etc.," a discourse, in short, on words, for all who use words to produce an effect upon the public. The outline was never filled out, but the existing fragments embody something of the author's insight into the relation between language and life and of his attitude as an artist towards his medium. The main theme bears a certain resemblance to Dante's unfinished treatise *On the Vulgar Tongue* and to Wordsworth's kindred prefaces. The language of books, Whitman saw, was not the language of the people, and, in so far as it was merely conventional, stood as a barrier between the writer and the world. He would have us realize that words are not original things, but accidents, transitory experiments of mankind in the nomenclature of emotions and ideas, and that all who deal publicly with expression must be co-workers in the confused and laborious process by which the new conceptions and the new moods of a nation find adequate symbols. The poet, too, must build upon something more basic than the word: "latent, in a great user of words, must actually be all passions, crimes, trades, animals, stars, God, sex, the past, night, space, metals, and the like — because these are the words, and he who is not these plays with a foreign tongue, turning helplessly to dictionaries and authorities." Such ideas are now not unfamiliar, but they were not current in New York in the fifties, and it is to Whitman's credit that he could evolve them, even thus blindly, for himself.

These great plans of interesting the public soon came to naught, however. His fertile imagination and his clear insight into the needs of the nation had tricked him into proposing for himself a course of action for which he had no real fitness or special training. It was not long before he came to see that he could not in this way press his message upon the attention of the public. Moreover, his mind was now becoming possessed by a new idea, — a new passion, one might say. Just as he had discovered for himself the immense social importance of man's love for woman, so now he was becoming aware of the fact that the love of man for man was the basic rock of democratic society.

For many years he had been strongly attracted to the stage-drivers of Broadway, men of a very special type, who had usually been bred in the country, and who had become expert in the extraordinarily difficult art, compounded of strength, skill, and intelligence, of managing a clumsy vehicle in a congested thorough-fare. Among his notes are a number of memoranda relating to such friends of his, in which it is apparent that at first he admired particularly in them their intense virility. With regard to Peter ——, for instance, he writes : —

" Peter ——, large, strong-boned young fellow, driver. Should weigh 180. Free and candid to me the very first time he saw me. Man of strong self-will, powerful coarse feelings and appetites. Had a quarrel, borrowed $300, left his father's somewhere in the interior of the State, fell in with a couple of gamblers, hadn't been home or written there in seven years. I liked his refreshing *wickedness*, as it would be called by the orthodox. He seemed to feel a perfect independence, dashed with a little resentment toward the world in general. I never met a man that seemed to me, as far as I could tell in forty minutes, more open, coarse, self-willed, strong and free from the sickly desire to be on society's lines and points."

As time wore on, however, we can dimly see that a new spirit entered into his relations with these and other men, a yearning, affectionate spirit. He was more drawn toward the younger men, who might have been his brothers or sons. His mystical imagination, which had at first been preoccupied with the over-powering sense of personal identity and with all that tended to magnify the individual and to make him virile and intense, and that hence centred itself largely in the life of the senses, was now being rapidly modified. He caught a glimpse of a new law — the good will and tender sympathy of man for man, on which all social progress might be said to rest. He began voluntarily to sacrifice himself for such men, to tend them in their sickness, and to comfort them in their afflictions; and in one instance he took a disabled driver's place for a whole winter, that his family might not lack its customary support. A similar tenderness and graciousness of feeling characterized his relationship with his friends among the ferry hands, as may be seen by the memories that one of them has put on record : —

" Thirty years ago, while employed upon an East River steamboat, I became acquainted with Walt Whitman, and the association has ever since been a treasured one by myself and the rest of my companion boatmen. He came among us simply as a sociable passenger, but his genial behavior soon made him a most welcome visitor. We knew somewhat of his reputation as a man of letters, but the fact made no great impression upon us, nor did he ever attempt a display of his gifts or learning that would in the least make us feel he was not ' of us, and one of us,' as he used to express it. In a charmingly practical demo-

G

cratic manner he took great pains to teach many valuable things
to a hard-handed band of men whose life had afforded little
time for books. In later years I have realized that ' Walt ' —
he would allow no other salutation from us — has done much
gratuitous work as a teacher, and in looking back I also realize
his excellence as an instructor. A careful choice of words and
terse method of explaining a subject were truly peculiar to
him — at least the faculty was marvellous to us. In our long
watches — he would pass entire afternoons and even nights
with us — he would discourse in a clear, conversational sort of
way upon politics, literature, art, music or the drama, from a
seemingly endless storing of knowledge. He certainly urged
some of us into a desire for attainments that perhaps would
not otherwise have been aroused. 'My boy,' he would often
say, after simply but eloquently treating some theme, ' you
must read more of this for yourself,' and then generously put
his library at the listener's service. I have seen a youth swab-
bing a steamboat's deck with Walt's Homer in his monkey-jacket
pocket ! "

A passage in the *Leaves of Grass* which was
written about this time, and which appeared only in
the edition of 1860, reveals the progress of his thought
under the spur of this new feeling. He was to sing
no more; he was to be the great comrade of man : —

" Long I thought that knowledge alone would suffice me — O if
    I could but obtain knowledge !
Then my lands engrossed me — Lands of the prairies, Ohio's
    land, the southern savannas, engrossed me — For them
    I would live — I would be their orator ;
Then I met the examples of old and new heroes — I heard of
    warriors, sailors, and all dauntless persons — And it
    seemed to me that I too had it in me to be as dauntless
    as any — and would be so ;
And then, to enclose all, it came to me to strike up the songs
    of the New World — And then I believed my life must
    be spent in singing ;

But now take notice, land of the prairies, land of the south
    savannas, Ohio's land,
Take notice, you Kanuck woods — and you Lake Huron —
    and all that with you roll toward Niagara — and you
    Niagara also,
And you Californian mountains — That you each and all find
    somebody else to be your singer of songs,
For I can be your singer of songs no longer — One who loves
    me is jealous of me, and withdraws me from all love,
With the rest I dispense — I sever from what I thought would
    suffice me, for it does not — it is now empty and tasteless
    to me,
I heed knowledge and the grandeur of the States, and the
    example of heroes, no more,
I am indifferent to my own songs — I will go with him I love,
It is to be enough for us that we are together — We never
    separate again."

Before his feeling reached the point where it
seemed that he should write no more, he had accumulated a considerable body of new poems, and in 1860
an opportunity to publish them presented itself.
Thayer and Eldridge, a Boston firm in good standing,
offered to reprint the *Leaves of Grass*, with whatever new material he had. Whitman accepted the
proposal, and in March of that year went to Boston to
superintend the setting-up of his book. There he
made a number of new friends, among them Mr.
Eldridge himself, whom he was later to know better
in Washington; W. D. O'Connor, a brilliant young
Irishman, whose Abolitionist novel, *Harrington*, was
soon to appear from the same press, and who afterwards became Whitman's stanch friend and champion; and J. T. Trowbridge, in whose reminiscences
there is an interesting record of the silent, gray-
haired, and gray-bearded poet, undemonstrative, and

without a touch of bravado or self-assertiveness, whom
he saw patiently correcting his proofs in a dingy
printing-office.

With Emerson he had a number of meetings, of one
of which he has left an interesting reminiscence :—

"Up and down this breadth by Beacon Street, between
these same old elms, I walk'd for two hours, of a bright sharp
February mid-day twenty-one years ago, with Emerson, then
in his prime, keen, physically and morally magnetic, arm'd at
every point, and when he chose, wielding the emotional just as
well as the intellectual. During those two hours he was the
talker and I the listener. It was an argument-statement, *recon-
noitring*, review, attack, and pressing home, (like an army
corps in order, artillery, cavalry, infantry,) of all that could be
said against that part (and a main part) in the construction
of my poems, ' Children of Adam.' More precious than gold to
me that dissertation — it afforded me, even after, this strange
paradoxical lesson ; each point of E.'s statement was unanswer-
able, no judge's charge ever more complete or convincing, I
could never hear the points better put — and then I felt down
in my soul the clear and unmistakable conviction to disobey all,
and pursue my own way. ' What have you to say then to such
things ? ' said E., pausing in conclusion. ' Only that while I
can't answer them at all, I feel more settled than ever to adhere
to my own theory, and exemplify it,' was my candid response.
Whereupon we went and had a good dinner at the American
House. And thenceforward I never waver'd or was touch'd
with qualms, (as I confess I had been two or three times before.")

Of the remaining important members of the Boston
group of men of letters he apparently saw little or
nothing. For Emerson he had the greatest respect
and affection, as for an elder and more austere brother
who did not deny the kinship of blood and spirit that
bound them both ; but between the others and him-

self there was little sympathy, and though Lowell printed Whitman's *As I ebb'd with the Ocean of Life* in the *Atlantic* for April, he does not seem to have taken advantage of this opportunity to seek Whitman's friendship. Father Taylor, however, the eloquent preacher at the Seamen's Bethel, Whitman heard often, recognizing him as the one "perfect orator" to whom he had ever listened; but here again there was a distant but distinct spiritual kinship.

The edition of 1860–1861 is a substantial volume, crowded with poems and parts of poems, new and old, the old bearing many marks of patient and skilful revision. It is a bewildering succession of moods, all expressed in Whitman's elusive fashion, a mass of sensations and symbols, from which it is impossible at first to gain definite or coherent impressions. One is stimulated in a multitude of ways, but it is only after repeated readings that it is possible to form a coherent and unified judgment.

As, however, reflection clarifies these glimpses into the heart of a great dreamer, one slowly begins to see how his mystic message was being transformed. The poet has ceased to wonder anew at the miracle of his own being; he has almost passed beyond his preoccupation with the stimuli of sex, though he collects and confirms his feelings on this topic before letting it drop entirely into the background of his thought. The message of equality, too, the mystic sympathy with all created things, though similarly confirmed, is scarcely so much stressed as in the previous poems, and though his mind runs much on the career of America and the proud democracy of labour which she is developing, his real thought lies deeper still. He

announces a new religion of affectionate comradeship
— a spiritual fellowship without which political and
industrial and physical democracy is of no avail: —

> " I dream'd in a dream, I saw a city invincible to the attacks
> of the whole of the rest of the earth;
> I dream'd that was the new City of Friends; nothing was
> greater there than the quality of robust love — it led the
> rest;
> It was seen every hour in the actions of the men of that city,
> And in all their looks and words."

Deeper yet, just as formerly his imagination had
dwelt exultantly on the passionate love of men and
women, to which our existence is due, so now it dwelt
on a second and greater law of love, — that force of
affection which, without stimulus of sex, binds humanity together: —

> " Fast-Anchor'd, eternal, O love! O woman I love!
> O bride! O wife! more resistless than I can tell, the thought of
> you!
> — Then separate, as disembodied, or another born,
> Ethereal, the last athletic reality, my consolation;
> I ascend — I float in the regions of your love, O man,
> O sharer of my roving life."

And deeper yet, in mystical broodings of fancy in
which few can follow him. Just as formerly he
pictured himself, as the type-man, as lover and husband and father, the incarnation of sex, so now he
announces himself as the lover of his friend, yearning
for his close companionship, for his kiss and his embrace. The Anglo-Saxon, with his sense of physical
aloofness, finds these sayings hard. Whitman himself falters and seems at times ill at ease, and declares
that he shades his thought; but it is clear that we

have here no abnormality or perversion of feeling. I should say rather that Whitman's extraordinary nature possessed to a most unusual degree, and with reference to many, the feeling of physical love, — wholly disassociated with sex, — which we, in varying degrees, bear to our parents, or brothers, or sons, or perhaps, more faintly, to friends. What appears to us as a minute, almost unrecognizable element in life, only revealing itself under exceptional circumstances, was to him a powerful and constant yearning, — the more so as he was cut off from his own children. Through his timid and hesitating expression of this new idea of physical comradeship one may perhaps catch a glimpse of the conception that a feeling so largely developed in him was merely latent in others ; and that in the evolution of our race there might become normal and natural in all men a yearning of companion for companion, a love of friend for friend, that would be among the highest manifestations of the divinity within us.

And deeper and more mystical still, a doctrine that as the love of sex was bound up with life, so this greater, more basic love was bound up with death. The former plays its part, fulfils its function, and has its end. The latter, less obvious in its aim, looks forward beyond the term of life for the fulfilment of its mysterious power. The love of sex wanes with age and disappears with life, but perhaps not so the other, which may somehow have the same affinity for death that its predecessor had for life. Whether Whitman was conscious of this inference is open to doubt, but the ideas appear in close juxtaposition in these poems, and seem to have had in his mind a real connection.

Such were the contents of the new volume issuing
from the press in the troubled days just preceding the
outbreak of the war. Even at a less perturbed moment his voice would scarcely have been heard by
many, and as it was misfortune early overtook the
venture. The political crisis came, and with it a re-
striction of credit. The publishing house failed, after
selling four or five thousand copies, and Whitman at
forty-two seemed destined to be a voice vainly crying
in the wilderness.

CHAPTER IV

WHITMAN returned from Boston in June, 1860, and resumed his quiet life in his mother's house, but we have little further information regarding him until late in 1862. When, in April, 1861, the Civil War broke out, Whitman's first thought must have been of what service he could render, for he was a zealous upholder of the Union, but he was obviously wise in not volunteering, and in biding his time until his proper duty revealed itself, though the possibility of entering the army remained in his mind long after he had become a hospital nurse. His slow ways and his unique individuality made him ill-suited for the discipline of camp and battle. His brother George, however, enlisted at once in the 51st New York Volunteers, and it was this circumstance that eventually changed the whole character of Whitman's life.

Few as are the data that bear on Whitman's life during this period of two years, we can surmise how much he was moved by the great turmoil about him. His dream of a brotherhood of American youth was apparently shattered forever, by civic strife, but he must have found hope in witnessing the exultant outburst of patriotism, and have been thrilled by the "drum-taps" to which the streets of Manhattan echoed as the troops gathered to the defence of their flag. For his own part he registered a vow, written in his own hand April 16, 1861, and found after his death, among his papers : " I have this day, this hour, resolved to inaugurate for myself a pure, perfect, sweet, clean-blooded, robust body, by ignoring all drinks but water and pure milk, and all fat meats, late suppers — a great body, a purged, cleansed, spiritualized, invigorated body." A frugal liver, he thus passed into something like austerity of diet, in discipline and in preparation for whatever call should be laid upon him.

This quiet life came to an end when, in December, 1862, his brother's name appeared in the list of those seriously wounded at Fredericksburg. Whitman at once started for Washington. His pocket was picked on the route, and he arrived penniless and without knowledge as to the whereabouts of his brother; but he was so fortunate as to find Mr. O'Connor, then in the Treasury Department, whom he had met in Boston, and who supplied him with funds and helped him to obtain information. George was not in the hospitals at Washington, and Whitman made his way with difficulty to the seat of war, where he found that his brother was already recovered from a wound in the cheek made by a fragment of a shell, and had just received his promotion to a captaincy. Once in camp, Whitman tarried a few days to see the life there, and, characteristically, became greatly interested in some of the sick and wounded men. Returning to Washington, he was, on the way, of much assistance in nursing them, and he determined to tarry awhile to see what further he could do for such unfortunates.

At that time Washington contained a whole city of sick and wounded men, perhaps fifty thousand or more, at first occupying public buildings already

standing — the vast area of the second story of the
Patent Office, for example, and even part of the Capitol, and afterward wooden one-story barracks. There
were fifty hospitals, each a little town in itself, full
of the wrecks of battle or disease. Camp sanitation
was little understood, and soldiers were wasted by
dysentery and fevers; antiseptic surgery had not been
discovered, and the mortality from suppurating wounds
was terrific; there was little provision on the part of
the Government; surgeons and nurses did what they
could, but, especially at first, there were many important
things left undone because there was no one to do
them. Particularly was this the case in respect to
the minor comforts of illness. The men were without
money, without news from their relatives, without
an opportunity of writing home; their major wants
were attended to, but they lacked comfort and inspiration and counsel. They died of homesickness and
abandonment. There were many in the Sanitary Service, and more particularly in the Christian Commission, who helped in such matters, and a few volunteers,
among whom Whitman was preëminent. He sup-
ported himself by a little newspaper work and by
copying a few hours each day in the office of Major
Hapgood, an army paymaster, where his friend and
former publisher, Mr. Eldridge, was now a clerk.
The greater part of his time he gave to the sufferers
in the hospitals. Friends in New York and elsewhere
supplied him with money for the work. Before the
war closed he had made about six hundred hospital
visits; cared, to a greater or less extent, for nearly a
hundred thousand unfortunates; and expended many
thousand dollars.

His methods were characteristic. When practicable
he prepared himself for his daily or nightly tour by
rest, a bath, and a hearty meal. Cheerful in appearance, quiet and slow in his movements, with apparently
an abundance of time for looking personally and carefully into whatever needed his attention, he was everywhere welcome. His theory was that personal affection
played a large part in therapeutics : —

" To many of the wounded and sick, especially the youngsters,
there is something in personal love, caresses, and the magnetic
flood of sympathy and friendship, that does, in its way, more
good than all the medicine in the world. I have spoken of my
regular gifts of delicacies, money, tobacco, special articles of
food, knick-knacks, etc., etc. But I steadily found more and
more that I could help, and turn the balance in favor of cure, by
the means here alluded to, in a curiously large proportion of
cases. The American soldier is full of affection and the yearning for affection. And it comes wonderfully grateful to him to
have this yearning gratified when he is laid up with painful
wounds or illness, far away from home, among strangers. Many
will think this merely sentimentalism, but I know it is the most
solid of facts. I believe that even the moving around among
the men, or through the ward, of a hearty, healthy, clean, strong,
generous-souled person, man or woman, full of humanity and
love, sending out invisible, constant currents thereof, does immense good to the sick and wounded.
" My custom is to go through a ward, or a collection of wards,
endeavoring to give some trifle to each, without missing any.
Even a sweet biscuit, a sheet of paper, or a passing word of
friendliness, or but a look or nod, if no more. In this way I go
through large numbers without delaying, yet do not hurry. I
find out the general mood of the ward at the time ; sometimes
see that there is a heavy weight of listlessness prevailing, and the
whole ward wants cheering up. I perhaps read to the men, to
break the spell, calling them around me, careful to sit away
from the cot of any one who is very bad with sickness or wounds.

Also I find out, by going through in this way, the cases that
need special attention, and can then devote proper time to them.
Of course, I am very cautious, among the patients, in giving
them food. I always confer with the doctor, or find out from
the nurse or ward-master about a new case. But I soon get
sufficiently familiar with what is to be avoided, and learn also
to judge almost intuitively what is best.''

His very appearance served to hearten men. As
he wrote to his mother : —

"I believe I weigh about 200, and as to my face, (so
scarlet,) and my beard and neck, they are terrible to behold.
I fancy the reason I am able to do some good in the hospitals
among the poor languishing and wounded boys, is that I am so
large and well — indeed like a great wild buffalo, with much
hair. Many of the soldiers are from the West, and far North,
and they take to a man that has not the bleached shiny and
shaved cut of the cities and the East.''

The best description of his work, however, came
from John Swinton : —

" I first heard of Whitman among the sufferers on the Peninsula after a battle there. Subsequently I saw him, time and
again, in the Washington hospitals, or wending his way there
with basket or haversack on his arm, and the strength of benefi-
cence suffusing his face. His devotion surpassed the devotion of woman. It would take a volume to tell of his kindness,
tenderness, and thoughtfulness.

" Never shall I forget one night when I accompanied him on
his rounds through a hospital, filled with those wounded young
Americans whose heroism he has sung in deathless numbers.
There were three rows of cots, and each cot bore its man.
When he appeared, in passing along, there was a smile of affection and welcome on every face, however wan, and his presence
seemed to light up the place as it might be lit by the presence
of the Son of Love. From cot to cot they called him, often in
tremulous tones or in whispers ; they embraced him, they
touched his hand, they gazed at him. To one he gave a few

words of cheer, for another he wrote a letter home, to others
he gave an orange, a few comfits, a cigar, a pipe and tobacco,
a sheet of paper or a postage stamp, all of which and many
other things were in his capacious haversack. From another
he would receive a dying message for mother, wife, or sweet-
heart ; for another he would promise to go on an errand ; to
another, some special friend, very low, he would give a manly
farewell kiss. He did the things for them which no nurse or
doctor could do, and he seemed to leave a benediction at every
cot as he passed along. The lights had gleamed for hours in
the hospital that night before he left it, and as he took his way
towards the door, you could hear the voice of many a stricken
hero calling, ' Walt, Walt, Walt, come again ! come again ! ' "

And the following incident, quoted by Dr. Bucke,
in his biography, from a writer in the New York
Tribune, is typical of the help he gave in scores or
hundreds of instances : —

" While walking in the neighborhood of New Rochelle, West-
chester County, a few days ago, I observed a man at work in
a field adjoining the road, and I opened a conversation with
him. He had served in the Union Army during the Rebellion,
and I had no trouble in inducing him to fight some of his
battles over again. He gave me a graphic description of how
he was badly wounded in the leg ; how the doctors resolved to
cut his leg off ; his resistance to the proposed amputation, and
his utter despair when he found he must lose his leg (as they
said) to save his life. As a last resort, he determined to appeal
to a man who visited the hospital about every alternate day.
This man was a representative of the Sanitary Commission
[this of course is a mistake], and he described him as a tall,
well-built man with the face of an angel. He carried over his
broad shoulders a well-filled haversack, containing about everything that would give a sick soldier comfort. In it were pens,
ink and paper, thread, needles, buttons, cakes, candy, fruit,
and above all, pipes and tobacco. This last article was in general demand. When he asked a poor fellow if he used tobacco
and the answer was ' no,' he would express some kind words

of commendation, but when the answer was ' yes,' he would
produce a piece of plug and smilingly say, ' Take it, my brave
boy, and enjoy it.' He wrote letters for those who were not
able to write, and to those who could he would furnish the
materials, and never forget the postage stamp. His good-
natured and sympathetic inquiry about their health and what
changes had taken place since he last saw them, impressed
every patient with the feeling that he was their personal friend.
To this man Rafferty (that was my informant's name) made
his last appeal to save his shattered leg. He was listened to
with attention, a minute inquiry into his case, a pause, and
after a few moments' thought the man replied, patting him on
the head, ' May your mind rest easy, my boy ; they shan't
take it off.' Rafferty began to describe his feelings when
he received this assurance, and though so many years have
passed since then, his emotions mastered him, his voice trem-
bled and thickened, his eyes filled with tears, he stopped for a
moment and then blurted out, slapping his leg with his hand,
' This is the leg that man saved for me.' I asked the name of
the Good Samaritan. He said he thought it was Whitcomb or
something like that. I suggested it was just like Walt Whitman. The name seemed to rouse the old soldier within him ;
he did not wait for another word from me, but seized my hand
in both of his, and cried, ' That's the man, that's the name ;
do you know him ? ' ' "

While carrying on such noble work, Whitman was
keeping his vow by living with new austerity. He occupied a little room in one lodging-house or another,
by preference near to the O'Connors, who had become
his fast friends. For some months they insisted on
his taking two meals a day with them ; afterwards he
shifted for himself, getting his own breakfast of toast
and tea, dining for a few cents at a humble restaurant,
and supping lightly in his own room. His personal
expenditures, always small, were now reduced to an
absolute minimum. His pleasures he took in such

walks in the vicinity as he could find opportunity for,
and in the society of the O'Connors, with whom he
often dined on Sundays, and around whom centred a
wholesome circle, which included C. W. Eldridge, his
former publisher, John Burroughs, and Edmund C.
Stedman, then clerks in the Government service. Between Whitman and Burroughs in particular there
sprang up a deep and lasting friendship. Thus passed
the years 1863 and 1864, and part of 1865, with the
exception of a month in the autumn of 1863 and the
whole latter part of 1864, when the state of his health
forced him back to Brooklyn for rest and recuperation.

In the midst of such labours there was no time for
literary composition, and his records of this period are
contained only in a few letters to the New York and
Brooklyn papers, in the many blood-stained and tear-
spotted little books in which he kept memoranda
about his patients, and in the few letters to his mother
which chanced to be preserved, and which were after
his death published by Dr. Bucke under the title of
The Wound Dresser. They were written in haste, in
a homely, unformed, almost illiterate fashion, revealing in every page the degree to which all attention to
style, all fineness and decoration of expression, were
being burnt out of the man in this crucible of passionate sympathy, leaving only the bare and crude statements of actual fact and feeling. But they were full
of tender affection for the aged mother, anxious for
George in the army and Walt in the hospital, for
Andrew dying of consumption, and Jeff with reduced
pay and seemingly on the point of being drafted.
His letters gave her good tidings of himself and
George, wise counsel about those at home, and tender

messages for his brothers and his sister and sisters-in-law, and the little niece he loved so much. One cannot read them without rich tribute to his sterling soundness and fineness of feeling and judgment.

Meanwhile his own magnificent health was breaking. Previously illness had been absolutely unknown to him. But the insufficient nourishment, the intense, moist heat of the Washington summers, indoor life, interrupted rest, poisonous contagion from wound dressing, were all draining his vigour. He was at one time infected through a cut in his hand, and the poison seems to have passed deeply into the enfeebled system. Malaria, too, had eaten into his good red blood. Worse perhaps than all was the sight of so much and such terrible suffering. Like most men who combine a phlegmatic exterior with a sensitive imagination, the after effects of his experiences were far greater than the immediate results. "It is curious," he wrote to his mother, "when I am present at the most appalling things — deaths, operations, sickening wounds (perhaps full of maggots) — I do not fail, although my sympathies are very much excited, but keep singularly cool; but often hours afterward, perhaps when I am home or out walking alone, I feel sick and actually tremble when I recall the thing and have it in my mind again before me." Again: "Mother, I see awful things. I expect one of these days, if I live, I shall have awful thoughts and dreams — but it is such a great thing to be able to do some real good; assuage these horrible pains and wounds, and save life even — that's the only thing that keeps a fellow up." And in other letters: "Mother, it seems not men, but a lot of devils and butchers, butchering one

H

another. . . . I get almost frightened at the world. . . .
Oh, it is terrible, and getting worse, worse, worse."
To this heart of love, indeed, the war was becoming
insupportable. To an ardent Abolitionist it was a war
for the liberation of a race, in which no sacrifice could
be too great; but Whitman saw only the frightful and
meaningless waste of life.

From time to time during the war Whitman thought
of his old scheme of lecturing. For himself, as he
wrote to his mother, "it don't seem to me it makes so
much difference about worldly successes (beyond just
enough to eat and drink and shelter, in the mod-
eratest limits) any more, since the last four months of
my life especially, and that merely to live, and have
one fair meal a day, is enough." But "I think something of commencing a series of lectures and reading,
etc., through different cities of the North, to supply
myself with the funds for my hospital and soldiers'
visits, as I do not like to be beholden to the medium of
others." Time and need pressed, however, and the
plan came to naught.

But he had not wholly forgotten his poems. He
asked his mother to look carefully after his papers,
"especially the copy of *Leaves of Grass* covered in
blue paper, and the little MS. book *Drum-Taps*, and
the MS. tied up in the square, spotted (stone-paper)
loose covers — I want them all carefully kept." In
his brief absence in Brooklyn, in November, 1863,
he wrote to Mr. Eldridge, "I feel to devote myself
more and more to the work of my life, which is making poems. I must bring out *Drum-Taps*. I *must*
be continually bringing out poems — now is the hey-
day — I shall range along the high plateau of my

life and capacity for a few years now, and then swiftly
descend. The life here in the cities, and the objects,
etc., of most, seem to me very flippant and shallow
somehow since I returned this time. . . ." And in
his convalescence in Brooklyn at the end of 1864, he
wrote again, " I intend to move heaven and earth to
publish my *Drum-Taps* as soon as I am able to go
around." Mr. Trowbridge, to whom he had read
parts of it, tried to find a publisher in Boston, but his
quest was unsuccessful, and finally Whitman undertook the volume at his own expense. It was printing in April, 1865, when the news came of Lincoln's
assassination. At once he set himself to the composition of *When Lilacs Last in the Dooryard Bloomed*
and *O Captain! my Captain!* and these with several
other verses he issued in a small supplementary
volume, *Sequel to Drum-Taps*, which appeared in
Washington late in the same year. Copies of it were
also bound up with the remainder of *Drum-Taps*.

Whitman himself was at that time inclined to
consider *Drum-Taps* as superior to *Leaves of Grass*,
"as a work of art and from the more simple and
winning nature of the subject and also because I have
in it only succeeded to my satisfaction in removing
all superfluity — verbal superfluity, I mean." "But,"
he continues in the same letter to Mr. O'Connor,
" I am perhaps mainly satisfied with *Drum-Taps* because it delivers my ambition of the task that has
haunted me, namely, to express in a poem (and in the
way I like, which is not at all by directly stating it),
the pending action of this *Time and Land we swim in*,
with all their large conflicting fluctuations of despair
and hope, the shiftings, masses, and the whirl and

deafening din (yet over all, as by an invisible hand, a
definite purport and idea), with the unprecedented
anguish of wounded and suffering, the beautiful young
men in wholesale death and agony, everything sometimes as if blood-color and dripping blood.   The book
is therefore unprecedently sad (as these days are, are
they not ?), but it also has the blast of the trumpet
and the drum pounds and whirrs in it, and then an
undertone of sweetest comradeship and human love
threads its steady thread inside the chaos and is heard
at every lull and interstice thereof.   Truly also, it has
clear notes of faith and triumph."

With this judgment all will, in the main, agree.
Not only is the subject-matter more simple and unified, but there is no trace of the turbulent spirit of the
earlier works, confessedly egotistic, exulting in the
consciousness of its just realized identity, insisting on
the necessity and sufficiency of carnal love.   Here is,
instead, a purified singer.   Only two short pieces of
the two little volumes, when Whitman redistributed
his verse, found their places among the *Children of
Adam*, and these are in essence farewells to love : —

"Out of the rolling ocean, the crowd, came a drop gently to
      me,
   Whispering, *I love you, before long I die,*
   I have travel'd a long way, merely to look on you, to touch you,
   For I could not die till I once look'd on you,
   For I fear'd I might afterward lose you.

" (Now we have met, we have look'd, we are safe ;
   Return in peace to the ocean, my love ;
   I too am part of that ocean, my love — we are not so much
      separated ;
   Behold the great rondure — the cohesion of all, how perfect!
   But as for me, for you, the irresistible sea is to separate us,

As for an hour, carrying us diverse — yet cannot carry us
    diverse forever;
Be not impatient — a little space — Know you, I salute the air,
    the ocean and the land,
Every day, at sundown, for your dear sake, my love.)

" I heard you, solemn-sweet pipes of the organ, as last Sunday
    morn I pass'd the church;
Winds of autumn! — as I walk'd the woods at dusk, I heard
    your long-stretch'd sighs, up above, so mournful,
I heard the perfect Italian tenor, singing at the opera —
    I heard the soprano in the midst of the quartet singing;
. . . Heart of my love! — you too I heard, murmuring low,
    through one of the wrists around my head;
Heard the pulse of you, when all was still, ringing little bells
    last night under my ear."

Moreover, the two volumes have an extraordinary
unity and completeness, in that they represent not
only the war itself as Whitman saw it, but the war in
its connection with the past and the future. It came to
him as from the clear sky, with inconceivable sudden-
ness and surprise. He had been dreaming of the
brotherhood of man, seeing only those signs of the
times that symbolized the drawing together of nations.
In the year of meteors, 1859-1860, he had seen the
wonderful *Great Eastern*, token of the increasing
facility of transportation; he had seen the crown
prince of England, token of amity and blood brotherhood with the East: —

"And you would I sing, fair stripling! welcome to you from
    me, sweet boy of England!
Remember you surging Manhattan's crowds, as you pass'd with
    your cortége of nobles?
There in the crowds stood I, and singled you out with attach-
    ment;

I know not why, but I loved you. . . . (And so go forth,
   little song,
Far over sea speed like an arrow, carrying my love all folded,
And find in his palace the youth I love, and drop these lines
   at his feet.)"

He had seen the first Japanese envoys: —

  "Over sea, hither from Niphon,
Courteous, the Princes of Asia, swart-cheek'd princes,
First-comers, guests, two-sworded princes,
Lesson-giving princes, leaning back in their open barouches,
   bare-headed, impassive,
This day they ride through Manhattan."

And both together he accepted as marking the place
that his country held and was to hold among the
powers of the world : —

" And you, Libertad of the world !
You shall sit in the middle, well-pois'd, thousands of years;
As to-day, from one side, the nobles of Asia come to you;
As to-morrow, from the other side, the Queen of England
   sends her eldest son to you.

" The sign is reversing, the orb is enclosed,
The ring is circled, the journey is done;
The box-lid is but perceptibly open'd — nevertheless the per-
   fume pours copiously out of the whole box."

From such dreamy hopes that humanity was " form-
ing en-masse," and that " the earth, restive, confronts
a new era," he is awakened by the imperious drums, —

'So strong you thump, O terrible drums — so loud you bugles
   blow, — "

that call the nation to arms : —

"Forty years had I in my city seen soldiers parading ;
    Forty years as a pageant — till unawares, the Lady of this
        teeming and turbulent city,
    Sleepless amid her ships, her houses, her incalculable wealth,
    With her million children around her — suddenly,
    At dead of night, at news from the south,
    Incens'd, struck with clench'd hand the pavement.

" A shock electric — the night sustain'd it;
    Till with ominous hum, our hive at day-break pour'd out its
        myriads.
    From the houses then, and the workshops, and through all
        the doorways,
    Leapt they tumultuous — and lo ! Manhattan arming."

But, instead of feeling himself perturbed by this
rude shattering of his humanitarian ideals, the poet is
thrilled by the thought that it is the real America
which he now beholds, an aroused America, North and
South.   He had long been sick of the petty super-
ficiality of city life : —

" The cities I loved so well, I abandon'd and left — I sped to
        the certainties suitable to me ;
    Hungering, hungering, hungering, for primal energies, and
        Nature's dauntlessness,
    I refresh'd myself with it only, I could relish it only ;
    I waited the bursting forth of the pent fire — on the water
        and air I waited long ;
    — But now I no longer wait — I am fully satisfied — I am
        glutted ;
    I have witness'd the true lightning — I have witness'd my
        cities electric ;
    I have lived to behold man burst forth, and warlike America
        rise ;
    Hence will I seek no more the food of the northern solitary
        wilds,
    No more on the mountains roam, or sail the stormy sea."

Indeed, the citizen soldier who surprised the world
by his bravery and endurance was the American he
had foreshadowed in his apotheosis of simple workmen
who, bound together by kinship and common interests,
constitute the state : " for who except myself have yet
conceiv'd what your children en-masse really are ? "

And then the war begins. There are brilliant
sketches of various scenes, finely and clearly drawn,
impressive in their simplicity and intensity : an army
corps on the march, cavalry crossing a ford, a
bivouac on a mountain side, a vigil by the dead on the
field of battle, an improvised hospital in the woods by
night, and those who have died for the redemption of
their fellows : —

" Then to the third — a face nor child, nor old, very calm, as
    of beautiful yellow-white ivory ;
Young man, I think I know you — I think this face of yours
    is the face of the Christ himself ;
Dead and divine, and brother of all, and here again he lies."

And, the war over, the poignant memories, the dread-
ful images, that perpetuate themselves in the minds
of those who have participated in the great conflict.
In the dead silence of the night, the artillery soldier,
lying wakeful at home, sees passing before his eyes all
the details of the engagement. The nurse, like Whitman himself, beholds again the long hospital wards : —

" Thus in silence, in dreams' projections,
Returning, resuming, I thread my way through the hospitals ;
The hurt and wounded I pacify with soothing hand,
I sit by the restless all the dark night — some are so young ;
Some suffer so much — I recall the experience sweet and sad ;
(Many a soldier's loving arms about this neck have cross'd
    and rested,
Many a soldier's kiss dwells on these bearded lips.)"

Thus, by successive movements, this great sym-
phony, the symbolic representation of the war, passes
to the finale, *President Lincoln's Burial Hymn*, —
strange and beautiful hymn, in which his name is not
mentioned, nor is there more than a faint reference to
him ; a threnody, therefore, of all that had died nobly
in the colossal struggle, symbolized through him. A
poem of three themes, it sings of the lilac blossoms,
sweet and homely and transient; of the evening star,
shining luminous for all men, but slowly sinking to its
rest; of the hermit thrush, Nature's one foreboding
singer of the wilderness at twilight. The flower of
the dooryard fades at the appointed time, the star
disappears according to its season, the bird sings of
death as the " deliveress " of mankind, for the poet's
trust is as strong as his love, and he contemplates
death with gratitude and with praise.

Further analysis fails. The poem lies almost in
the realm of music, but scarcely more so than many
or most of those contained in the two joined volumes.
They present the war without reference to space or
time. There is no mention of North or South, of
purpose or result, of slavery or freedom, of states'
rights or nationalism. All Whitman saw and suffered
is transmuted into a symphonic tragedy, purging
the soul of pity and fear by the excitation of these
same passions, and leaving it full of hope and tenderness.

Last of all we find the one personal note in the
volumes. Whitman's self-sacrifice was not without
its effect. He found himself the better soldier,
pledged anew to a warfare with his weaker self : —

" Ah poverties, wincings, and sulky retreats !
Ah you foes that in conflict have overcome me !
(For what is my life, or any man's life, but a conflict with
    foes — the old, the incessant war ?)
You degradations — you tussle with passions and appetites ;
You smarts from dissatisfied friendships, (ah wounds, the
    sharpest of all ;)
You toil of painful and choked articulations — you mean-
    nesses ;
You shallow tongue-talks at tables, (my tongue the shallowest
    of any ;)
You broken resolutions, you racking angers ; you smother'd
    ennuis ;
Ah, think not you finally triumph — My real self has yet to
    come forth ;
It shall yet march forth o'ermastering, till all lies beneath
    me ;
It shall yet stand up the soldier of unquestion'd victory."

Early in 1863 Whitman had secured letters of recom-
mendation to prominent politicians, with the inten-
tion of applying for a clerkship in some Government
bureau, planning to support himself by such labour
while continuing his work in the hospitals. He had
interviews with some of these men, but was impressed
by the difficulty of obtaining an appointment, and de-
sisted from his efforts. Late in the same year, Mr.
Trowbridge, who was staying in Washington as the
guest of Secretary Chase, discovered that Whitman
had letters from Emerson to Chase and Seward, and
at once took up the matter with his host, who, while
welcoming Emerson's letter for the sake of the autograph, thought it impossible to give a clerkship to a
man who had written a " notorious " book. In 1865,
however, Whitman made a formal application, and
was, in February, assigned a position in the Indian

Bureau of the Department of the Interior, where he
had a few hours of work each day, good pay, and could
still continue his hospital visits in his leisure hours.
During his short time of service a large deputation of
Indians visited Washington, greatly to the delight of
Whitman, who observed them carefully, and later
made interesting memoranda of the impression made
upon him by their physical grace, dignity, and beauty.

In June, the Secretary of the Interior, James Harlan,
learned that Whitman had in his desk an immoral book.
This was a copy of the *Leaves of Grass* which
Whitman was revising for a new edition. After the
office was closed for the day, therefore, Mr. Harlan
opened Whitman's desk, examined the book, came to
the conclusion that it contained indecent passages, and
curtly notified Whitman, on June 30, that from and
after that date his services would be dispensed with.
No reason was given.

Whitman himself would naturally have been unwilling to apply for reinstatement under such circumstances, but his friends were indignant and not
disposed to let the matter drop. Mr. J. H. Ashton, then
assistant United States attorney, went personally to
Mr. Harlan in protest. The Secretary acknowledged
that Whitman performed his duties faithfully and com-
petently, but, on the evidence of the book, declared him
to be an immoral man. Mr. Ashton, who had known
Whitman for some years, was easily able to show him
how far he had misjudged Whitman's character; but
though convinced on this point, Mr. Harlan was firm
in his refusal to have in his department the author of
the *Leaves of Grass*. Mr. Ashton, however, was fortunately able to procure the immediate transfer of

Whitman to his own department, and the incident
seemed closed. Outside Washington it had attracted
no attention.

Whitman's impetuous friend O'Connor was, however,
not content to let what seemed to him an act of great
injustice pass unpunished, and he determined to appeal
to the sympathy of the public. In a brilliant, eloquent,
and even learned pamphlet, dated September 2, 1865,
but not published until several months later, he held
the offending official up to the scorn of the beholder.
It was the work of an orator rather than a man of
letters — a tirade, a philippic, a torrent of burning
words, in which the love of sound tended to overpower
the judgment. The title — *The Good Gray Poet* —
was a happy inspiration. He began by describing the
poet's picturesque and beneficent aspect, — "the flowing hair and fleecy beard, both very gray, and temper-
ing with a look of age the youthful aspect of one
who is but forty-five," — and went on to relate Lincoln's
exclamation on first seeing him ("Well, *he* looks like
a *Man*"), the instinctive trust and admiration shown
him by men of the people, and his services during the
war. Then he narrated the incidents connected with
Whitman's discharge by Mr. Harlan, and Mr. Harlan's
defence that he was the author of an indecent and immoral book. That the *Leaves of Grass* was nothing
of the sort he attempted to show negatively by citing
a multitude of the great authors of antiquity and of
the renaissance, all containing passages to which Mr.
Harlan would object. If you stamp Whitman as indecent, he maintained, you must extend the condemnation to pretty much every author of reputation up to
very recent times.

The issue thus raised was unfortunately fated for a
long time to hold the attention of the critic and the
public whenever Whitman's name was mentioned. For
many years the conflict was heated though intermittent.
Not only Mr. Harlan, but the great majority of readers,
held the simple doctrine that all allusions to sexual congress were excluded from publicity, and hence from
literature. Such things were *tacenda*. Other races and
other times had other customs, and they admitted the
blots on many a fair page of earlier literature ; but they
would countenance no more improprieties. O'Connor's
negative defence laid Whitman open to a wholly false
impression by tacitly classing him with the licentious
authors of the renaissance. For an essential difference
at once strikes the thoughtful reader of to-day, namely,
that Whitman's audacious references, his apotheosis of
physical love, are not licentious or lascivious; they
deal with the subject, not slyly, but boldly; not mirth-
fully, but seriously and solemnly. From this point of
view, the opposite doctrine has come in the course of
half a century to be simply that under certain circumstances art may admit such topics; that they are not
always *tacenda*, but may sometimes be *canenda*. But
this change of attitude on the part of a minority was
long in coming, as was the feeling that the topic did
not by any means involve the whole of Whitman's art;
and in the meantime Whitman's friends were not much
helping his cause by their ill-advised defence on these
lines.

In the remainder of the famous little pamphlet,
O'Connor was on surer ground. He describes the book
positively instead of negatively, and hails it as the
beginning of a new movement in American literature.

His praise is extravagant in both form and substance, but time is justifying in the main his double claim that Whitman's was a new way, and that he was a forerunner in that he wrote, to a large degree, spontaneously, without foreign models, and on purely American subjects, in contrast, for example, with Longfellow, — though O'Connor does not make the comparison, — who often wrote on American subjects, but who had found his methods of treatment to a large extent in foreign literature, and whose acquaintance with his native country was obviously so slight as scarcely to make him a special representative of it. Here again the contest of opposing views was to be spirited, but it was productive of many good results, and the consensus of opinion is slowly shaping itself, with many limitations, along the lines of O'Connor's argument, from which we quote briefly : —

" What is this poem, for the giving of which to America and the world, and for that alone, its author has been dismissed with ignominy from a Government office ? It is a poem which Schiller might have hailed as the noblest specimen of naïve literature, worthy of a place beside Homer. It is, in the first place, a work purely and entirely American, autochthonic, sprung from our own soil ; no savor of Europe nor of the past, nor of any other literature in it ; a vast carol of our own land, and of its Present and Future ; the strong and haughty psalm of the Republic. There is not one other book, I care not whose, of which this can be said. I weigh my words and have considered well. Every other book by an American author implies, both in form and substance, I cannot even say the European, but the British mind. The shadow of Temple Bar and Arthur's Seat lies dark on all our letters. Intellectually, we are still a dependency of Great Britain, and one word — colonial — comprehends and stamps our literature. In no literary form, except our newspapers, has there been anything distinctively American. . . .

This literature has often commanding merits, and much of it is very precious to me ; but in respect to its national character, all that can be said is that it is tinged, more or less deeply, with America ; and the foreign model, the foreign standards, the foreign ideas, dominate over it all.

" At most, our best books were but struggling beams ; behold in *Leaves of Grass* the immense and absolute sunrise ! It is all our own ! The nation is in it ! In form a series of chants, in substance it is an epic of America. It is distinctively and utterly American. Without model, without imitation, without reminiscence, it is evolved entirely from our own polity and popular life."

O'Connor's hero-worshipping crusade was not immediately productive of good results. It told in the long run, for it helped to set the issues squarely before the public; but it made few converts, and the comments of the press and of critics were, generally speaking, unfavourable. The old charges were again brought forward, though there was noticeable a growing warmth of personal feeling towards Whitman, and a disposition to acknowledge many merits in his verse. The most interesting reply which the pamphlet called forth was the following characteristic letter from Matthew Arnold : —

ATHENEUM CLUB, PALL MALL, S.W.,
Sept. 16, 1866.

" DEAR SIR, — I have been absent from London for some months, and on my return I find your note of the 4th of June with the two books you have been good enough to send me. Their predecessors, which you mention, I do not find.

" Mr. Harlan is now, I believe, out of office, but had he still remained in office I can imagine nothing less likely to make him reconsider his decision respecting your friend than the interference of foreign expostulators in the matter. I have read your statement with interest, and I do not contest Mr. Walt

Whitman's powers and originality. I doubt, however, whether here, too, or in France, or in Germany, a public functionary would not have had to pay for the pleasure of being so outspoken the same penalty which your friend has paid in America. As to the general question of Mr. Walt Whitman's poetical achievements, you will think that it savours of our decrepit old Europe when I add that while you think it is highest merit that he is so unlike anyone else, to me this seems to be his demerit; no one can afford in literature to trade merely on his own bottom and to take no account of what the other ages and nations have acquired : a great original literature America will never get in this way, and her intellect must inevitably consent to come, in a considerable measure, into the European movement. That she may do this and yet be an independent intellectual power, not merely as you say an intellectual colony of Europe, I cannot doubt; and it is on her doing this, and not on her displaying an eccentric and violent originality that wise Americans should in my opinion set their desires.

" With many thanks for the good will towards me which you express, I am, dear sir,

" Very faithfully yours,

" MATTHEW ARNOLD."

W. D. O'CONNOR, ESQ.,
  Washington, D.C.,
    United States.

Meanwhile Whitman was living quietly as a Government clerk of the third class, drawing sixteen hundred dollars a year, — a large sum for him, or at that time for any man of simple tastes. Some of his salary he had put in the savings bank ; the residue, after his regular expenses were met, went to his hospital work, to his friends, or to beggars, for whom he always had a few pennies. His work was not arduous, and he was free from great responsibility and the necessity of initiative. His desk was by the window in the Treasury Building, with a charming view over the river,

and he often spent the evening reading in his office.
He lived in a comfortable boarding-house. After his
day's work was over and on holidays, he took long
and leisurely walks in the country, and he rode much
on the horse-cars. On Sundays it was his custom to
breakfast with Mr. and Mrs. Burroughs and to take
tea with the O'Connors ; between the two visits he
made, until the end of 1866, a little hospital round.
It was a quiet, thoughtful, leisurely life, a period in
which to rest after the strain of the preceding years,
and to store up energy for the next emergency — soon
to come — in which it would be required.

His circle of friends and acquaintances among
people of distinction was by no means small, and
among ordinary folk it was very large indeed. Such
friends knew little or nothing about his writings, but
they liked him and his unobtrusive ways. Indeed, he
had become in a sense a public character, partly on
account of his striking appearance and unusual attire,
but mainly because he was felt instinctively to be, as
it were, the friend of every one. He had, moreover, a
set of friends in what we might call the other world,
the world of working people, a world into which few
of us actually penetrate except by proxy. John Burroughs has recorded a characteristic incident of those
days : —

"I give here a glimpse of him in Washington on a Navy
Yard horse car one summer day at sundown. The car
is crowded and suffocatingly hot, with many passengers
on the rear platform, and among them a bearded, florid-
faced man, elderly, but agile, resting against the dash, by
the side of the young conductor, and evidently his intimate
friend. The man wears a broad-brim white hat. Among the
jam inside near the door, a young Englishwoman, of the work-

I

ing class, with two children, has had trouble all the way with the youngest, a strong, fat, fretful, bright babe of fourteen or fifteen months, who bids fair to worry the mother completely out, besides becoming a howling nuisance to everybody. As the car tugs around Capitol Hill the young one is more demoniac than ever, and the flushed and perspiring mother is just ready to burst into tears with weariness and vexation. The car stops at the top of the Hill to let off most of the rear platform passengers, and the white-hatted man reaches inside and gently but firmly disengaging the babe from its stifling place in the mother's arms, takes it in his own, and out in the air. The astonished and excited child, partly in fear, partly in satisfaction at the change, stops its screaming, and as the man adjusts it more securely to his breast, plants its chubby hands against him, and pushing off as far as it can, gives a good long look squarely in his face — then as if satisfied snuggles down with its head on his neck, and in less than a minute is sound and peacefully asleep without another whimper, utterly fagged out. A square or so more and the conductor, who has had an unusually hard and uninterrupted day's work, gets off for his first meal and relief since morning. And now the white-hatted man, holding the slumbering babe also, acts as conductor the rest of the distance, keeping his eye on the passengers inside, who have by this time thinned out greatly. He makes a very good conductor, too, pulling the bell to stop or go on as needed, and seems to enjoy the occupation. The babe meanwhile rests its fat cheeks close on his neck and gray beard, one of his arms vigilantly surrounding it, while the other signals, from time to time, with the strap ; and the flushed mother inside has a good half hour to breathe, and cool, and recover herself.''

By such open-hearted kindness and friendliness Whitman endeared himself to working-men, who recognized in him at once a kindred spirit. The most notable of these friendships was that with Peter Doyle, a simple, manly, and affectionate mechanic, thirty years younger than Whitman, a homeless soldier of the Confederacy, who, freed in Washington on parole, became a street-car conductor. He has himself told the story of his first meeting with Whitman : —

"I was a conductor. The night was very stormy, — he had been over to see Burroughs before he came down to take the car — the storm was awful. Walt had his blanket — it was thrown round his shoulders — he seemed like an old sea-captain. He was the only passenger, it was a lonely night, so I thought I would go in and talk with him. Something in me made me do it and something in him drew me that way. He used to say there was something in me had the same effect on him. Anyway, I went into the car. We were familiar at once — I put my hand on his knee — we understood. He did not get out at the end of the trip — in fact went all the way back with me. I think the year of this was 1866. From that time on we were the biggest sort of friends. . . . Walt rode with me often — often at noon, always at night. He rode round with me on the last trip — sometimes rode for several trips. Everybody knew him. He had a way of taking the measure of the drivers' hands — had calf-skin gloves made for them every winter in Georgetown — these gloves were his personal presents to the men. He saluted the men on the other cars as we passed — threw up his hand. They cried to him, ' Hullo, Walt ! ' and he would reply, ' Ah, there ! ' or something like. He was welcome always as the flowers in May. Everybody appreciated his attentions, and he seemed to appreciate our attentions to him."

Whitman formed not a few such friendships, but that with Doyle was the most intimate and the most enduring. He loved him as a father, and the young man responded with a son's affection. Always at night Whitman joined Doyle on his car for the last trip of the day, and after that was over they supped together, and sat long in a restaurant, talking not of books but of the simple things of life, or talking not

at all. "Like as not," said Doyle in his affectionate
reminiscences, "I would go to sleep — lay my head on
my hands on the table. Walt would stay there, wait,
watch, keep me undisturbed — would wake me up
when the hour of closing came. . . . We took great
walks together [particularly on moonlight nights] —
off towards or to Alexandria, often. We went plodding
along the road, Walt always whistling or singing.
We would talk of ordinary matters. He would recite
poetry, especially Shakspere. He was always active,
happy, cheerful, good-natured."

When Whitman was away on his vacations he wrote
Doyle at short intervals, and by good fortune these
missives were preserved by Doyle, and, after Whitman's death, were published by Dr. Bucke, one of
Whitman's executors, under the appropriate title of
Calamus. The letters are simplicity itself, and reveal
not so much a side of Whitman's character as another
personality. It is amazing to consider that this really
great thinker and poet, capable of discussing subjects
of national or universal importance with grasp and
acuteness, should be capable of so lowering, so to
speak, his threshold of consciousness as to dwell in an
infantile world of little happenings and of primitive
emotions. At such times he is another man — writing
crudely, feeling crudely, not so much putting himself
in the place of the humble workman as actually becoming such. The following extract is typical: —

"*Brooklyn, September* 2, 1870. Dear Pete. I received your
welcome letter of Aug. 27th and also 31st, enclosing Ned Stew-
art's — when you write tell Ned I am here in Brooklyn, loafing
around — and that I send my love. Pete, there is nothing particular to write about this time — pretty much the same story

— every day out on the bay awhile, or going down to Coney
Island beach — and every day from two to four or five hours in
the printing office — I still keep well and hearty, and the
weather is fine — warm through the middle of the day, and
cool morning and nights — I fall in with a good many of my
acquaintances of years ago — the young fellows, (now not so
young) — that I knew intimately here before the war — some
are dead — and some have got married — and some have grown
rich — one of the latter I was up with yesterday and last night
— he has a big house on Fifth Avenue I was there to — dinner
(dinner at 8 P.M.!) — everything in the loudest sort of style,
with wines, silver, nigger waiters, etc. etc. etc. But my friend
is just one of the manliest, jovialest, best sort of fellows — no
airs, and just the one to suit you and me, — no women in the
house — he is single — he wants me to make my home there —
I shall not do that, but shall go there very frequently — the
dinners and good wines are attractive — then there is a fine
library. Well, Pete, I am on the second month of my furlough
— to think it is almost six weeks since we parted there that
night — my dear loving boy, how much I want to see you — it
seems a long while. I have received a good letter from Mr.
O'Connor, and also one from John Rowland who is in the office
for me. Nothing new in office — Well, Pete, about half of our
separation is over — the next six weeks will soon pass away —
indeed it may be only four, as John Rowland told me he might
wish to go away — Good-bye for the present, my loving son,
and give my respects to any of the boys that ask about me.
WALT."

Another letter shows more plainly his deep affection.   Doyle had been ill, and was in so despondent a
condition that he had hinted at suicide : —

" Dearest boy, I have not a doubt but you will get well and
entirely well — and we will one day look back on these draw-
backs and sufferings as things long past. The extreme cases
of that malady, (as I told you before) are persons that have
very deeply diseased blood so they have no foundation to build
on — you are of healthy stock, with a sound constitution and

good blood — and I know it is impossible for it to continue
long. My darling, if you are not well when I come back I will
get a good room or two in some quiet place, and we will live together and devote ourselves together to the job of curing you, and
making you stronger and healthier than ever. I have had this
in my mind before but never broached it to you. I could go on
with my work in the Attorney General's office just the same —
and we would see that your mother should have a small sum every
week to keep the pot a-boiling at home. Dear comrade, I
think of you very often. My love for you is indestructible, and
since that night and morning has returned more than before.
Dear Pete, dear son, my darling boy, my young and loving
brother, don't let the devil put such thoughts in your mind
again — wickedness unspeakable — death and disgrace here, and
hell's agonies hereafter — Then what would it be afterward to the
mother ? What to *me* ? — Pete, I send you some money by
Adams' Express — you use it, dearest son, and when it is gone
you shall have some more, for I have plenty. I will write
again before long — my love to Johnny Lee, my dear darling
boy. I love him truly — (let him read these three last lines) —
Dear Pete, *remember* — WALT."

While in one personality Whitman was a humble
son of the people, without apparent motive beyond
the simple enjoyment of life and the fulfilment of its
daily duties of labour, and in another was the Government clerk with a circle of well-dressed friends,
contented in his little routine, and without special
interest in literature, he was, in a third personality,
separated widely from either of the others, meditating
deeply on high problems and singing nobly of them.
In 1871 he wrote a long poem, *After All, not to
create Only*, for the opening of the fortieth exhibi-
tion of the American Institute, a forerunner of the
many "expositions" of later days. It treated antiquity with somewhat rough humour, and implored the
muse to desert her ancient haunts, leave her worn-out

themes, placard "removed" and "let" on Parnassus,
and realize that there are better spheres and a wider
domain for her rule. But this jocose passage is
atoned for by that which follows, a glowing summary
of all that was most beautiful in a past now

"Pass'd to its charnel vault — laid on the shelf — coffin'd, with
    crown and armor on,
Blazon'd with Shakspeare's purple page,
And dirg'd by Tennyson's sweet sad rhyme."

The sphere for the muse is now in the democracy of the
New World, with its rich industrial life and its hope
of healthful and happy citizens.

In 1871, too, appeared a new edition of the *Leaves
of Grass*, with many slight changes and improve-
ments, and with the addition of a group of remarkable
poems centring around the *Passage to India*, which
were also published separately. The new edition
turned to democracy for its keynote: "One's Self I
sing — a simple, separate person; yet after the word
Democratic, the word *En-masse*." The elder genius of
poetry declared to him that the muse should sing of
war : —

" Be it so, then I answer'd,
    I too, haughty Shade, also sing war — and a longer and
    greater one than any."

But it was the great war of man with himself, as he
rises to higher freedom, a war for the "old cause!
Thou peerless, passionate good cause!"

In the little group of poems centring around the
Passage to India, we find Whitman at his highest level
of composition. They are, in the main, short, highly
musical in phrasing, and begin always with splendidly

sonorous lines; the rhythm is strong, flexible, and
well sustained, and there is a marked tendency to the
use of the refrain.   They are, too, readily intelligible,
so far as any poems can be intelligible which express
their meaning by symbols alone, or rather use symbols
for the purpose of creating an affective mood of great
range and intensity.   They deal almost entirely with
the larger aspirations of the soul, and the symbolism
continually used is that of the ship or the bird questing on strong pinions.

The *Passage to India* itself was suggested by
the opening of the Suez Canal and of the railroads
across this continent.   Physically speaking, the barriers of the world were thus demolished, leaving humanity free for comradeship : —

> "Lo, soul ! seest thou not God's purpose from the first ?
> The earth to be spann'd, connected by net-work,
> The people to become brothers and sisters,
> The races, neighbors, to marry and be given in marriage,
> The oceans to be cross'd, the distant brought near,
> The lands to be welded together.
>
> "(A worship new, I sing;
> You captains, voyagers, explorers, yours!
> You engineers! you architects, machinists, yours!
> You, not for trade or transportation only,
> But in God's name, and for thy sake, O soul.)"

His fancy dwelt with delight, moreover, on the long
line of adventurous spirits who had striven to burst
these barriers, the ancient traders, the mediæval
travellers and merchants, the valorous explorers of
the renaissance, — a whole magnificent group of
pioneers and visionaries.   All these are but symbols

of the adventures of the soul, its continual flight into the unseen, its passionate voyaging towards God: —

" Reckoning ahead, O soul, when thou, the time achiev'd,
(The seas all cross'd, weather'd the capes, the voyage done,)
Surrounded, copest, frontest God, yieldest, the aim attain'd,
As, fill'd with friendship, love complete, the Elder Brother
    found,
The Younger melts in fondness in his arms."

The minor poems of the group repeat in different keys the same theme, dwelling, as in *Whispers of Heavenly Death*, on the setting free of the soul from the body : —

" I see, just see, skyward, great cloud-masses ;
Mournfully, slowly they roll, silently swelling and mixing ;
With, at times, a half-dimm'd, sadden'd, far-off star,
Appearing and disappearing.
(Some parturition, rather—some solemn, immortal birth :
On the frontiers, to eyes impenetrable,
Some Soul is passing over.)"

Or, under the favourite symbol of the ship and the sailor, they sing of voyagers saying farewell before departing on the great quest, as in *Now Finale to the Shore*, and in

" Joy ! shipmate — joy !
(Pleas'd to my Soul at death I cry;)
Our life is closed — our life begins ;
The long, long anchorage we leave,
The ship is clear at last — she leaps !
She swiftly courses from the shore ;
Joy ! shipmate — joy ! "

In 1871, too, Whitman published his first body of prose, *Democratic Vistas*, a set of linked meditations on the fortunes of democracy in America, on

which he had been working for several years. They
follow the lines suggested by him in his earlier prefaces, but they are also somewhat in the nature of a
commentary on Carlyle's *Shooting Niagara, and After*,
which had appeared in 1867. Carlyle's rough-
and-ready condemnation of American democracy had
at first roused Whitman's wrath, but reflection had
shown him certain similarities between their ideas.
Carlyle found practical democracy a failure and believed in the sterner rule, secured somehow, of the
aristos, the really *best* man. And this *aristos* will be
sometimes " speculative, speaking or vocal," the hero as
poet or prophet or priest, who will deliver the truth
to mankind. He will not be the mere man of letters,
with his silly verse or fiction, but one who can teach
the public what liberty really means and lead it in
paths of wisdom and high ideals. Whitman, though
not doubtful of the material success of the democracy,
was, no less than Carlyle, alive to the slightness of its
progress on higher lines : —

   "The depravity of the business classes of our country is not
less than has been supposed, but infinitely greater. The official
services of America, national, state, and municipal, in all their
branches and departments, except the judiciary, are saturated
in corruption, bribery, falsehood, maladministration ; and the
judiciary is tainted. The great cities reek with respectable as
much as non-respectable robbery and scoundrelism. In fashionable life, flippancy, tepid amours, weak infidelism, small aims,
or no aims at all, only to kill time. In business, (this all-de-
vouring modern word, business,) the one sole object is, by any
means, pecuniary gain. The magician's serpent in the fable ate
up all the other serpents ; and money-making is our magician's
serpent, remaining to-day sole master of the field. The best
class we show is but a mob of fashionably dress'd speculators
and vulgarians. True, indeed, behind this fantastic farce,

enacted on the visible stage of society, solid things and stupen-
dous labors are to be discover'd, existing crudely and going on in
the background, to advance and tell themselves in time. Yet
the truths are none the less terrible. I say that our New
World democracy, however great a success in uplifting the
masses out of their sloughs, in materialistic development,
products, and in a certain highly-deceptive superficial popular
intellectuality, is, so far, an almost complete failure in its social
aspects, and in really grand religious, moral, literary, and
esthetic results. In vain do we march with unprecedented
strides to empire so colossal, outvying the antique, beyond
Alexander's, beyond the proudest sway of Rome. In vain have
we annex'd Texas, California, Alaska, and reach north for
Canada and south for Cuba. It is as if we were somehow being
endow'd with a vast and more and more thoroughly-appointed
body, and then left with little or no soul."

To free the citizen from conscienceless greed much
was necessary. He must be led to higher ideals.
Nothing would help us more than that the states, " with
all their variety of origins," should possess " an aggregate of heroes, characters, exploits, sufferings, prosperity or misfortune, glory or disgrace, common to all,
typical of all." Nothing is really of value except
" the fervid and tremendous Idea," — the true basis
of nationality. To realize that high common feeling,
we must insist on perfect individualism, the " simple
idea that the last, best dependence is to be upon
humanity itself, and its own inherent, normal, full-
grown qualities, without any superstitious support
whatever." It was the people in whom he believed,
the common stock, and the common stock does not
so much need learning and culture as it does con-
science and religion and comradeship. To gain such
basic qualities he has, in essence, only two means to
suggest. First, the physical race must be strong and

fine, and this is a question of good fatherhood and motherhood. Second, the race must be roused to spiritual activity by a new group of poets and orators : —

"Then still the thought returns, (like the thread-passage in overtures,) giving the key and echo to these pages. When I pass to and fro, different latitudes, different seasons, beholding the crowds of the great cities, New York, Boston, Philadelphia, Cincinnati, Chicago, St. Louis, San Francisco, New Orleans, Baltimore — when I mix with these interminable swarms of alert, turbulent, good-natured, independent citizens, mechanics, clerks, young persons — at the idea of this mass of men, so fresh and free, so loving and so proud, a singular awe falls upon me. I feel, with dejection and amazement, that among our geniuses and talented writers or speakers, few or none have yet really spoken to this people, created a single image-making work for them, or absorb'd the central spirit and the idiosyncrasies which are theirs — and which, thus, in highest ranges, so far remain entirely uncelebrated, unexpress'd.

"Dominion strong is the body's ; dominion stronger is the mind's. What has fill'd, and fills to-day our intellect, our fancy, furnishing the standards therein, is yet foreign. The great poems, Shakspere included, are poisonous to the idea of the pride and dignity of the common people, the life-blood of democracy. The models of our literature, as we get it from other lands, ultramarine, have had their birth in courts, and bask'd and grown in castle sunshine ; all smells of princes' favors. Of workers of a certain sort, we have, indeed, plenty, contributing after their kind ; many elegant, many learn'd, all complacent. But touch'd by the national test, or tried by the standards of democratic personality, they wither to ashes. I say I have not seen a single writer, artist, lecturer, or what not, that has confronted the voiceless but ever erect and active, pervading, underlying will and typic aspiration of the land, in a spirit kindred to itself. Do you call those genteel little creatures American poets ? Do you term that perpetual, pistareen, paste-pot work, American art, American drama, taste, verse ? I think I hear, echoed as from some mountain-top afar in the west, the scornful laugh of the Genius of these States."

Whitman's ideas thus have much in common with
Carlyle's. Both men were profoundly dissatisfied
with existing conditions ; both looked to literature
to right the wrongs of the present; both felt greatly
rather than reasoned well; both wrote with high enthusiasm, in an involved, oratorical, many-coiled style,
forever winding back to a few simple ideas. The
difference lay mainly in the constitutional, perhaps
physical, contrast of temperament between the opti-
mist and the pessimist. Like Plato, Whitman saw a
vision of the perfect state, and yearned for its attain-
ment, and he believed heartily that the grand common
stock, each man and woman well begotten and well
nurtured, conscious of his own identity, inspired by
great poets to high comradeship, would one day gain
the victory over itself. But that victory, as he said
in his noble closing passage, would not be without toil,
nor without the aid of the poet : —

" Even to-day, amid these whirls, incredible flippancy, and
blind fury of parties, infidelity, entire lack of first-class captains
and leaders, added to the plentiful meanness and vulgarity of
the ostensible masses — that problem, the labor question, beginning to open like a yawning gulf, rapidly widening every
year — what prospect have we ? We sail a dangerous sea of
seething currents, cross and under-currents, vortices — all so
dark, untried — and whither shall we turn ? It seems as if the
Almighty had spread before this nation charts of imperial destinies, dazzling as the sun, yet with many a deep intestine
difficulty, and human aggregate of cankerous imperfection, —
saying, lo ! the roads, the only plans of development, long and
varied with all terrible balks and ebullitions. You said in your
soul, I will be empire of empires, overshadowing all else, past
and present, putting the history of old-world dynasties, con-
quests behind me, as of no account — making a new history, a
history of democracy, making old history a dwarf — I alone

inaugurating largeness, culminating time. If these, O lands of
America, are indeed the prizes, the determinations of your
soul, be it so. But behold the cost, and already specimens of
the cost. Thought you greatness was to ripen for you like a
pear ? If you would have greatness, know that you must con-
quer it through ages, centuries — must pay for it with a pro-
portionate price. For you too, as for all lands, the struggle,
the traitor, the wily person in office, scrofulous wealth, the sur-
feit of prosperity, the demonism of greed, the hell of passion, the decay of faith, the long postponement, the fossil-like
lethargy, the ceaseless need of revolutions, prophets, thunder-
storms, deaths, births, new projections and invigorations of
ideas and men.

" Yet I have dream'd, merged in that hidden-tangled problem of our fate, whose long unraveling stretches mysteriously
through time — dream'd out, portray'd, hinted already — a little
or a larger band — a band of brave and true, unprecedented
yet — arm'd and equipt at every point — the members separated, it may be, by different dates and States, or south, or
north, or east, or west — Pacific, Atlantic, Southern, Canadian
— a year, a century here, and other centuries there — but always one, compact in soul, conscience-conserving, God-incul-
cating, inspired achievers, not only in literature, the greatest
art, but achievers in all art — a new, undying order, dynasty,
from age to age transmitted — a band, a class, at least as fit to
cope with current years, our dangers, needs, as those who, for
their times, so long, so well, in armor or in cowl, upheld and
made illustrious, that far-back feudal, priestly world. To
offset chivalry, indeed, those vanish'd countless knights, old
altars, abbeys, priests, ages and strings of ages, a knightlier
and more sacred cause to-day demands, and shall supply, in a
New World, to larger, grander work, more than the counterpart and tally of them."

In June, 1872, at the invitation of the United Literary Societies, Whitman delivered *As a Strong Bird
on Pinions Free* as the Commencement poem at Dartmouth College. The invitation is said to have origi-

nated in a boyish joke, somewhat lacking in courtesy, on
the part of the students, who, perhaps bearing in mind
the *Children of Adam,* wished to embarrass their elders
by the choice of a poet whose personality and whose per-
formance would be the subject of mirth.   If such were
the case, their hopes were disappointed, for Whitman
bore himself with quiet dignity, and his poem, though
not well read, was a noble and patriotic utterance, fore-
telling the joys of the new democracy.   From Hanover,
the rural peace of which was doubly delightful to one
coming from Washington, he journeyed to Burlington,
Vermont, to visit his sister Hannah and thence back
to Brooklyn.   The Dartmouth poem, with the *Mystic
Trumpeter* and several others, was issued the same
year in a little pamphlet, together with a preface along
the same general lines as those of *Democratic Vistas.*
He followed, too, his old custom of spreading correct
ideas about his own work, by writing an able review
of the pamphlet.   The conclusion shows the calm and
sensible way in which he regarded himself: —

"Time only can show if there is indeed anything in them.
This Walt Whitman — this queer one whom most of us have
watched, with more or less amusement, walking by — this goer
and comer, for years, about New York and Washington — good-
natured with everybody, like some farmer, or mate of some
coasting vessel, familiarly accosted by all, hardly any one of us
stopping to Mr. him — this man of many characters, among the
rest that of volunteer help in the army hospitals and on the field
during the whole of the late war, carefully tending all the
wounded he could, southern or northern — if it should turn out
that in this plain unsuspected old customer, dressed in gray and
wearing no neck-tie, America and her republican institutions are
possessing that *rara avis* a real national poet, chanting, putting
in form, in her own proud spirit, in first class style, for present
and future time, her democratic shapes even as the bards of

Judah put in song, for all time to come, the Hebrew spirit, and
Homer the war-life of pre-historic Greece, and Shakspere the
feudal shape of Europe's kings and lords !

" Whether or not the future will justify such extravagant
claims of his admirers, only that future itself can show. But Walt
Whitman is certainly taking position as an original force and
new power in literature.   He has excited an enthusiasm among
the republicans and young poets of Europe unequalled by our
oldest and best known names.   The literary opposition to him
in the United States has, it is true, been authoritative, and continues to be so.   But the man has outlived the stress of misrep-
resentation, burlesque, evil prophecy, and all calumnies and im-
putations, and may now answer, as Captain Paul Jones did,
when, after the onslaught of the Serapis, he was asked if he had
struck his colors — ' Struck ? ' answered the Captain quietly,
' not at all — I have only just begun my part of the fighting.' "

We may smile, if we choose, at the unconventionality
of his undertaking to comment in this anonymous way
on his own work, and at the odd phrases which he
employs, but what he said was true.   He had outlived much misunderstanding ; he was still undefeated
and confident of eventual victory ; he was, in his way,
" a real national poet."

Though Whitman had been so active in composition,
the condition of his health was far from satisfactory.
In August, 1869, while on his vacation, he had written
to Peter Doyle that he had been ill for several days:
" I don't know what to call it — it makes me prostrated
and deadly weak, and little use of my limbs."   A fortnight later he wrote that he felt ill " most every day
— some days not so bad.   Besides I have those spells
again, worse, last longer, sick enough, come sudden,
dizzy and sudden sweat. — It is hard to tell exactly
what is the matter or what to do.   The doctor says it
is all from that hospital malaria, hospital poison ab-

sorbed in the system years ago." As the years passed
by these attacks tended to increase, and during the
night of January 23, 1873, he awoke to find that he
could not move his left arm and leg. Characteristically,
he went off to sleep again; but in the morning his
condition was the same, and it was evident that he
had suffered a slight attack of paralysis.

His friends came at once to his assistance. The
Ashtons would have had him removed to their house,
but, as he wrote to his mother, " They live in grand
style and I should be more bothered than benefited by
their refinements and luxuries, servants, etc." He
added, " Mother, I want you to know truly that I do
not want for anything — as to all the *little extra fixings*
and *superfluities*, I never did care for them in health,
and they only annoy me in sickness— I have a good
bed — as much grub as I wish and whatever I wish
— and two or three good friends here."

The paralysis was slight and yielded slowly to good
treatment. Meanwhile Doyle, Eldridge, and Burroughs took turns in caring for him, and Mrs. O'Connor
came often to do little acts of kindness. At no time
did he lose control of his intellectual faculties; he
soon began to occupy himself with reading and composition; and he sent to his mother, at short intervals,
affectionate and sensible letters, not disguising the
truth, but showing that he took his illness bravely and
hopefully. In a few weeks he was about his room, and
early in April he began regularly to work at his office for
a couple of hours each day. Early in May, however,
Mrs. Whitman, who was living with George at Camden,
New Jersey, became seriously ill, and he hastened
to her bedside, arriving in time to be present at her

K

death. The bond between them had been peculiarly strong and the shock was great, and was intensified by the decease, shortly before, of his sister-in-law, Martha, Jeff's wife, who had been a great favourite of his. Weakened by his illness, his journey, the hot weather, which at that time affected him unusually, and by his grief, he succumbed again to a more severe attack of paralysis, which brought an end to his clerk's life at Washington. He was fifty-four and was destined to live nearly twenty years longer. As we shall see, he later recovered his strength to an astonishing degree and did notable work in his old age; but he was now to pass through a period of illness and poverty which might well have broken even his confident spirit. His poems had expressed the glad aspirations of his soul at the thought of quick release from the body, but he was now to be long tied to a crippled self, and all his optimism was to be tested to the full.

This is an appropriate place, however, to speak of the cheering effect upon him, in 1866 and the years immediately following, of the markedly greater appreciation of his work at home and abroad. In 1867 the New York *Times* had accepted a laudatory review of the new edition of the *Leaves of Grass* by O'Connor, and *The Galaxy* issued a similar article by Burroughs; and Burroughs also published an interesting little biography, the first of many, entitled *Notes on Walt Whitman as Poet and Person*. In June, 1868, moreover, there appeared in *Putnam's Magazine* a short but remarkable work of prose fiction called *The Carpenter*, by O'Connor. No mention is made of Whitman's name or work, but the chief character of the story is plainly drawn from him, and is the first

expression of the extraordinary feeling of reverent
affection with which many persons regarded Whitman
in his middle and later life. He had over them an
inexplicable influence, comfort-giving, strength-bear-
ing, such as might come from divinity itself. The
tale has to do with Christmas Eve in a farm-house in
Pennsylvania at the time of the war. All preparations have been made for a festival, but discord and
sorrow hang heavily over the family. The father
knows himself to be bankrupt; the mother mourns
her youngest son, who has fled from home to fight in
the Southern army; the eldest son, just returned from
the Northern army, is tortured by jealousy, and his
wife, finding him stern, is drawn more than ever to a
younger and more sympathetic man; and he in his
turn, egotistic and light-hearted, stands hovering on
the edge of a sinful passion. A knock is heard at
the door, and there enters a traveller seeking shelter
for the night. " He was tall and stalwart, with uncovered head; a brow not large, but full, and seamed
with kindly wrinkles; a complexion of rosy clearness; heavy-lidded, firm blue eyes, which had a stead-
fast and draining regard; a short, thick, gray beard
almost white, and thinly-flowing dark-gray hair. His
countenance expressed a rude sweetness. He was
dressed in a long, dark overcoat, much worn, and of
such uncertain fashion that it almost seemed a gab-
ardine. As he stood there in the gracious darkling
light, he looked an image of long and loving experi-
ance with men, of immovable composure and charity,
of serene wisdom, of immortal rosy youth in reverend
age. A faint perfume exhaled from his garments.
In the lapel of his coat he wore a sprig of holly. His

left hand, in which he also held his shapeless hat,
carried a carpenter's plane."

The influence of the wayfarer is almost immediate.
Each member of the family feels strongly attracted to
him, and to each he shows at once his affection and
his comprehension of the other's difficulties. He had
nursed both sons in the hospitals, and now he recon-
ciles the younger with his father and the elder with
his wife; the wife's lover he rebukes and then in-
structs him how to turn his genius for affection to
noble uses; and even the father's financial difficulties
he disperses by his calm and intelligent grasp of the
situation. Then, leaving a happy household behind
him, he departs into the night as abruptly as he came,
and the crippled little grandchild whose pain he has
assuaged declares him in her childish fancy to be the
good Christ Himself. The conception was a daring
one, and in other hands it would have provoked either
laughter or indignation; but O'Connor's skill was
equal to the occasion, and the narrative is so full of
tenderness that the reader finds it neither irreverent
towards God nor overbold in its idealization of man.

Copies of the earlier editions of the *Leaves of Grass*
had been sent abroad, but they had apparently fallen
for the most part on barren soil. It was otherwise
with the edition of 1867, which was favourably re-
viewed in Germany in the *Allegemeine Zeitschrift* in
1868, by Freiligrath, who, accustomed through Wagner
to the idea of a freer method of musical composition,
was inclined to a similar open-mindedness in regard
to verse. In England there were favourable notices
also, and the book fell into the hands of the younger
men of letters, Swinburne, W. M. Rossetti, F. W.

Myers, Symonds, Dowden, and others, who, for rea-
sons somewhat diverse, were eclectic in their tastes
and disposed to welcome good poetry, in whatever
garb it was attired. These men were all deeply moved
by Whitman. "My academical prejudices," wrote
Symonds some years later, "the literary instincts
trained by two decades of Greek and Latin studies,
the refinements of culture, and the exclusiveness of
aristocratic breeding, revolted against the uncouthness,
roughness, irregularity, coarseness of the poet and his
style. But in the course of a short time, Whitman
delivered my soul of these debilities. . . . *Leaves of
Grass,* which I first read at the age of twenty-five, influenced me more perhaps than any other book has
done, except the Bible; more than Plato, more than
Goethe. . . . I do not think it is a religion only for
the rich, the powerful, the wise, the healthy. For my
own part, I may confess that it shone upon me when
my life was broken, when I was weak, sickly, poor,
and of no account; and that I have lived thenceforward in the light and warmth of it."

This spontaneous recognition of Whitman as a poet
soon became evident in literature. In 1868 appeared
Swinburne's essay on Blake, at the close of which he
points out " sides of likeness many and grave " between Blake and Whitman : —

"To each the imperishable form of a possible and universal
Republic is equally requisite and adorable as the temporal and
spiritual queen of ages as of men. They are both full of faith
and passion, competent to love and to hate, capable of contempt
and of worship. The divine devotion and selfless love which
makes men martyrs and prophets are alike visible and palpable
in each. And in externals and details the work of these two
constantly and inevitably coheres and coincides. A sound as

of sweeping wind ; a prospect as over dawning continents at
the fiery visitant of a sudden sunrise ; a splendour now of stars
and now of storms ; an expanse and exultation of wing across
strange spaces of air and above shoreless stretches of sea . . .
a strength and security of touch in small sweet sketches of
colour and outline, which bring before the eyes of their student
a clear glimpse of the thing designed — some little inlet of sky
lighted by moon or star, some dim reach of windy water or
gentle growth of meadow-land or wood ; these are qualities
common to the work of either."

Later in the same year also, there appeared a volume
of selections from Whitman's poems, edited by W. M.
Rossetti, and intended exclusively for English readers.
Rossetti had been for some time in correspondence
with Whitman and his friends in regard to the delicate question of expurgation.   The publisher was unwilling to print the complete edition, which might
have laid him open to prosecution, and Whitman was
unwilling to permit in England what he had refused
to allow at home ; the matter was settled by Whitman's giving leave to Rossetti to choose such poems
as he pleased, but to publish these in full.

Rossetti's interest in Whitman was certainly genuine,
and in his preface to the selections he declared the
Leaves of Grass to be "incomparably the largest per-
formance of our period in poetry," and prophesied
that Whitman's " voice will one day be potential or
magisterial wherever the English language is spoken."
There were, however, limitations : he objected to the
grossness of Whitman's language and the grossness of
the ideas he sometimes expressed, to his absurd and
ill-constructed words; to the peculiarities of his style,
in particular to his method of agglomeration; and to
his boundless (though often vicarious) self-assertion.

Such limitations, shared by many of Whitman's early admirers in England, showed that they were far from understanding thoroughly the relation that these matters bore to his theory of art; but, whatever limitation Rossetti set on his praise of Whitman, his selections served to make the poet known to a small but important set of readers in Great Britain, and formed for some years the central point of the movement, if such it may be called, in Whitman's favour.

Essays and reviews of Whitman now appeared more frequently, the most remarkable of these being an article in the *Westminster Review* for July, 1871, by Edward Dowden, the first critic to seize the essence of Whitman's theory and to present it intelligently. Swinburne addressed a poem to Whitman in his *Songs before Sunrise* (1871); Tennyson wrote him twice, in terms of fraternal affection, as one monarch might address another; Rudolf Schmidt, who had written on Whitman in a Danish literary journal, translated *Democratic Vistas* into Danish, and sent him a message from Björnson; and a multitude of pleasant relationships were thus little by little established.

The greatest and most delightful tribute which Whitman received at this period was one of a sort wholly unexpected. Mrs. Anne Gilchrist, who, after her husband's death, completed with much skill and learning his life of Blake, was a friend of Rossetti's, and becoming acquainted with the *Selections*, felt impelled to read the complete edition of the *Leaves of Grass*. In asking Rossetti to lend her the volume, she wrote quite frankly that, " as for what you specially allude to, who so well able to bear it — I will say, to judge wisely of it — as one who, having been a

happy wife and mother, has learned to accept with
tenderness, to feel a sacredness in all the facts of
nature?" "But," she adds, "perhaps Walt Whitman
has forgotten — or, thro some theory in his head,
has overridden — the truth that our instincts are
beautiful facts of nature, as well as our bodies, and
that we have a strong instinct of silence about some
things." A few days later, having received and read
the poems, she wrote Rossetti thus courageously about
them : —

"11 *July*. I think it was very manly and kind of you to put
the whole of Walt Whitman's poems into my hands ; and that I
have no other friend who w'd have judged them and me so
wisely and generously. . . . In regard to those poems which
raised so loud an outcry, I will take courage to say frankly that
I find them also beautiful, and that I think even you have mis-
apprehended them. Perhaps indeed they were chiefly written
for wives. I rejoice to have read these poems ; and if I or any
true woman feel that, certainly *men* may hold their peace about
them. You will understand that I still think that instinct of
silence I spoke of a right and beautiful thing ; and that it is
only lovers and poets (perhaps only lovers and *this* poet) who
may say what they will — the lover to his own, the poet to all
because all are in a sense his own. Shame is like a very flexible
veil that takes faithfully the shape of what it covers — lovely
when it hides a lovely thing, ugly when it hides an ugly one.
There is not any fear that the freedom of such impassioned
words will destroy the sweet shame, the happy silence, that
enfold and brood over the secrets of love in a woman's heart."

With Mrs. Gilchrist's consent, her letters were sent,
without mention of her name, to Whitman, and a
little later they were published in the Boston *Radical*
under the title of *A Woman's Estimate of Walt Whitman.* Their influence in decreasing the attacks on
Whitman for indecency of expression is scarcely to

be exaggerated. When once a woman of refinement had declared that the wife and mother understood his meaning and was not shocked by it, the ground was, as it were, cut out from under the prudish male critic. At the same time, the limitations which she placed upon her admiration defended her from any imputation of recklessness in opening wide the realm of song for the indiscriminate admission of poems that dealt with love in this fashion.

In general, however, the effect of foreign appreciation of Whitman's work on the home public was not considerable. Indeed, American readers and critics were both inclined to underrate the value of such judgments from afar, classing them with such ill-informed opinion as fancied that Indians in their war-paint still roamed in the outskirts of the great Eastern cities, and that the typical American of the cultivated class was portrayed in Dickens's *American Notes*. They forgot, nevertheless, that to the English reader verse or prose that merely represented the continuation of English tradition seemed naturally worthy of no special remark, and that while the majority of American writers, particularly perhaps those from New England, were living under conditions not easily to be distinguished from English conditions, and writing much as Englishmen would, there was throughout the world a deep interest in such American writing as represented conditions more widely national. America, Europe has steadily felt, is the great modern experiment in democracy, the pioneer in the mastery of a huge continent; she attempts the assimilation of many races; her peoples are living on a new basis, they are facing new problems, — their life must have in it something suggestive of all these. What thoughtful Europeans heard most gladly from us, therefore, was not the speech of the sophisticated, the virtually Europeanized literary class, but the speech of the people at large, the song of democracy. And though Whitman did not write in a way that could often be understood by the people, he spoke *of* them and, in a great measure, *for* them.

CHAPTER V

OLD AGE (1873–1892)

CAMDEN in New Jersey, where Whitman was to spend the greater part of the remaining years of his life, lies on the opposite side of the Delaware from Philadelphia, of which it may be regarded as a suburb. Colonel Whitman was an inspector of gas and water pipes, and his family occupied a comfortable house, in which Whitman had the room formerly used by his mother. In September, the Whitmans moved to a larger and more pleasantly situated house, where Whitman chose for himself a chamber on the top floor. His relatives were kind to him and saw carefully to all his needs. But he was far from happy. He was partly disabled by paralysis and got about only with difficulty. His brother had little time to spend in convoying his slow steps, and he had as yet no friends or even acquaintances. In addition to his paralysis, he suffered from gastric catarrh or some obstinate affection of the liver, brought on, he thought, by his unaccustomed sedentary life and confinement indoors. His brain, too, was often in a " blur," as he expressed it. His Washington friends could only come to see him at rare intervals, and he was lonely and depressed, missing his old wood fire (the house was heated in a more modern fashion), and finding it hard work to get through the long evenings.

We know most of his life during 1873–1875 through

139

his letters to Peter Doyle, to whom he wrote frequently in the old colloquial, fragmentary, almost illiterate fashion. He confesses to him how much he misses his "friendly presence and magnetism" and warns him that, though "I still think I shall get over this, and we will be together again and have some good times, for all that it is best for you to be prepared for something different — my strength can't stand the pull forever, and if continued must sooner or later give out." As a rule, however, he is hopeful and declares that he puts a bold face on and his best foot foremost. His main longing was for companionship; close by were men of the sort that he liked — "lots of R. R. [railroad] men living near, around here — if only I felt just a little better I should get acquainted with many of the men, which I could very easily do if I would. I should much like to go on the trips so handy and cheap, right as you might [say] from my door, to Cape May, or to Long Branch, etc. If you was only here to convoy me — but I suppose no one is to have *everything*." And so he plans for the welfare of his "dear son," dreams of returning to Washington soon, and sends messages of affection to one and another of his humble friends.

For a year Whitman was allowed to perform his Washington duties by proxy, but when, in the midsummer of 1874, it became evident that his return would be postponed indefinitely, he received his discharge. Up to this time he had been meeting his expenses from his savings and the residue of his salary. Now that the latter was cut off and his savings were vanishing, his financial situation began to look black, for the sale of his books was small, and

even the slight sums that should have reached him
from them were withheld by dishonest agents, who
seemed to think that his death would soon relieve
them from an accounting. His physical condition
slowly improved. He got out of doors more, and once
able to reach the horse-car lines, he had long rides,
crossed the ferry to Philadelphia, and took the cars
on the other side. The drivers gave him their little
stools on the forward platforms, and the ferrymen
welcomed him cordially. Late in 1875 he even made
a brief visit to Washington, "convoyed" by Burroughs,
and, with Doyle, to Baltimore, where he attended the
ceremonies at the reburial of Poe's body. But these
years were, all in all, the most lonely and miserable
period of his life.

Of literary composition, during this time, he was
almost absolutely incapable ; yet we owe to it at
least three poems : *The Song of the Universal*, read
by proxy at Tufts College at Commencement, in
1874, on the thought that "only the good is universal," and that in America, in particular, the plan
of God is slowly bringing men to a larger hope and
reality; *The Song of the Redwood Tree*, the dying
message of the dryads of the mighty forests of the
Pacific coast, majestic giants passing away because
their time had come, abdicating, as it were, to a
superber race, in the new and promised land of freedom and true democracy ; and, best of all, the magnificent *Prayer of Columbus*, published in *Harper's
Monthly*. In this he symbolizes his own condition.
Columbus, " a batter'd, wreck'd old man," long pent
by the sea, on a savage shore, reports himself once
more to God : —

"Thou knowest my years entire, my life,
   My long and crowded life of active work, not adoration merely;
   Thou knowest the prayers and vigils of my youth,
   Thou knowest my manhood's solemn and visionary meditations,
   Thou knowest how before I commenced I devoted all to come
      to Thee,
   Thou knowest I have in age ratified all those vows and strictly
      kept them,
   Thou knowest I have not once lost nor faith nor ecstasy in Thee,
   In shackles, prison'd, in disgrace, repining not,
   Accepting all from Thee, as duly come from Thee. . . .

"The end I know not, it is all in Thee,
   Or small or great I know not — haply what broad fields,
      what lands,
   Haply the brutish measureless human undergrowth I know,
   Transplanted there may rise to stature, knowledge worthy
      Thee,
   Haply the swords I know may there indeed be turn'd to
      reaping-tools,
   Haply the lifeless cross I know, Europe's dead cross, may
      bud and blossom there.

" One effort more, my altar this bleak sand ;
   That Thou, O God, my life hast lighted,
   With ray of light, steady, ineffable, vouchsafed of Thee,
   Light rare untellable, lighting the very light,
   Beyond all signs, descriptions, languages ;
   For that, O God, be it my latest word, here on my knees,
   Old, poor, and paralyzed, I thank Thee."

In 1876, however, the tide of fortune began to turn.
In his few working hours he had been able to prepare
for the press a new edition of the *Leaves of Grass*, the
sixth, and a companion volume, *Two Rivulets*, — that
is, twin streams of prose and verse, respectively, —
containing *Democratic Vistas*, the new prose *Memoranda
of the War*, and such poems as had been written since
the previous edition of the *Leaves of Grass*. The two

volumes sold at five dollars each. Before they were
actually published, a letter from Robert Buchanan
appeared in the London *News,* accusing Americans of
neglecting Whitman, who was old and ill and in want.
The charge was, from some points of view, unjust,
but it moved W. M. Rossetti to write to Whitman,
offering the assistance of his English friends. Whitman replied (March 17, 1876) that he was no worse,
and might remain for years in the same condition.
He added: —

" My books are out, the new edition ; a set of which, immediately on receiving your letter of 28th, I have sent you, (by
mail, March 15,) and I suppose you have before this receiv'd
them. My dear friend, your offers of help, and those of my
other British friends, I think I fully appreciate, in the right
spirit, welcome and acceptive — leaving the matter altogether
in your and their hands, and to your and their convenience,
discretion, leisure, and nicety. Though poor now, even to penury,
I have not so far been deprived of any physical thing I need
or wish whatever, and I feel confident I shall not in the future.
During my employment of seven years or more in Washington
after the war (1865-72) I regularly saved part of my wages :
and, though the sum has now become about exhausted by my
expenses of the last three years, there are already beginning at
present welcome dribbles hitherward from the sales of my new
edition, which I just job and sell, myself, (all through this illness, my book-agents for three years in New York successively,
badly cheated me,) and shall continue to dispose of the books
myself. And *that* is the way I should prefer to glean my support. In that way I cheerfully accept all the aid my friends find
it convenient to proffer.

" To repeat a little, and without undertaking details, understand, dear friend, for yourself and all, that I heartily and most
affectionately thank my British friends, and that I accept their
sympathetic generosity in the same spirit in which I believe
(nay, know) it is offer'd — that though poor I am not in want

— that I maintain good heart and cheer ; and that by far the
most satisfaction to me (and I think it can be done, and believe
it will be) will be to live, as long as possible, on the sales, by
myself, of my own works, and perhaps, if practicable, by further
writings for the press.   W. W.

"I am prohibited from writing too much, and I must make
this candid statement of the situation serve for all my dear
friends over there."

Rossetti took steps to circulate this information
among Whitman's friends in Great Britain, and the
result was a handsome subscription for the two volumes, some of the subscribers voluntarily paying for
the books double the stated price. To Whitman these
remittances came just in time to free him from serious
financial inconvenience. "These blessed gales from
the British isles probably (certainly) saved me," he
said; and he had the happiness not only of knowing
that he was loved and helped by his friends, but that
the receipts were derived from his own labours.

Feeling by this time somewhat better in body, and
surer now of financial independence, he was able to
lead a less secluded and monotonous life. In the
spring of 1876 he accordingly left Camden for the
village of Whitehorse, some ten miles away, where he
lodged in an old farm-house, with the family of Mr.
George Stafford. The country is gently rolling, well
timbered, and full of rich meadowland. The farm
lay far from the main roads, and near by was Timber
Creek, a placid branch of the Delaware. The farm-
house was comfortable, his hosts became his warm
friends, country life agreed with him, and he remained
until late in the autumn, returned for the following
summer, and in fact made the Staffords' house one of
his homes for several years.

He lived much in the open air, his chief resort being "a particularly secluded little dell off one side
by the creek, originally a large dug-out marl-pit, now
abandon'd, fill'd with bushes, trees, grass, a group of
willows, a straggling bank, and a spring of delicious
water." Here he gave himself up to the medicine of
air and water and exercise. For several hours each
day he enjoyed the mud-bath of the creek and the
clear bath of the brook, and the friction of a flesh-
brush. He basked in the sun, and wrestled with a
young hickory sapling, swaying and yielding to its
tough, limber stem, "haply to get into my old sinews
some of its elastic fibre and clear sap. . . . Wandering by the creek, I have three or four naturally favor-
able spots where I rest — besides a chair I lug with me
and use for more deliberate occasions. At other spots
convenient I have selected, besides the hickory just
named, strong and limber boughs of beech or holly, in
easy-reaching distance, for my natural gymnasia, for
arms, chest, trunk-muscles. I can soon feel the sap
and sinew rising through me, like mercury to heat. I
hold on boughs or slender trees caressingly there in
the sun and shade, wrestle with their innocent stal-
wartness — and *know* the virtue thereof passes from
them into me. . . . How it is I know not, but I often
realize a presence here — in clear moods I am certain
of it, and neither chemistry nor reasoning nor esthet-
ics will give the least explanation. All the past two
summers it has been strengthening and nourishing my
sick body and soul, as never before. Thanks, invisible physician, for thy silent delicious medicine, thy
day and night, thy waters and thy airs, the banks, the
grass, the trees, and e'en the weeds!"

L

In the years immediately following this happy
change of fortune we see Whitman at his very best.
No longer in financial anxiety, comparatively free from
bodily pain, with faculties not yet dimmed by old age,
with powers of enjoyment undiminished, he seemed
at the very height of his powers. The reminiscences
of Dr. Bucke and Edward Carpenter, who came to
know him at this period, are of great interest as showing the growth in him of a peculiar physical or
psychic power, felt keenly by certain persons, less
perceptibly by others, and by some not at all.

Dr. Bucke records of their first meeting that he was
"almost amazed by the beauty and majesty of his
person and the gracious air of purity that surrounded
and permeated him." The interview was short, but
shortly after it " a sort of spiritual intoxication set
in. . . . It seemed to me at that time certain that he
was either actually a god or in some sense clearly and
entirely præter-human. Be all this as it may, it is
certain that the hour spent that day with the poet was
the turning point of my life." Elsewhere he describes
a similar experience of another person, — an exaltation
that " lasted at least six weeks in a clearly marked
degree, so that, for at least that length of time, he
was plainly different from his ordinary self. Neither,
he said, did it then or since pass away, though it
ceased to be felt as something new and strange, but
became a permanent element in his life, a strong and
living force (as he described it), making for purity
and happiness. I may add that this person's whole
life has been changed by that contact (no doubt the
previous reading of *Leaves of Grass* also), his temper,
character, entire spiritual being, outer life, conversa-

tion, etc., elevated and purified in an extraordinary
degree." Indeed, "no description," Dr. Bucke af-
firms, "can give any idea of the extraordinary physical attractiveness of the man. I do not speak now of
the affection of friends and of those who are much
with him, but of the magnetism exercised by him
upon people who merely see him for a few minutes or
pass him on the street. An intimate friend of the
author's, after knowing Walt Whitman a few days,
said in a letter: 'As for myself, it seems to me now
that I have always known him and loved him.' And
in another letter, written from a town where the poet
had been staying for a few days, the same person
says: 'Do you know, every one who met him here
seems to love him?'"

Edward Carpenter's testimony lies in the same
direction : —

"Meanwhile in that first ten minutes I was becoming conscious of an impression which subsequently grew even more
marked — the impression, namely, of immense vista or background in his personality. If I had thought before (and I do
not know that I had) that Whitman was eccentric, unbalanced,
violent, my first interview certainly produced quite a contrary
effect. No one could be more considerate, I may almost say
courteous; no one could have more simplicity of manner and
freedom from egotistic wrigglings; and I never met any one who
gave me more the impression of *knowing what he was doing*
than he did. Yet away and beyond all this I was aware of a
certain radiant power in him, a large benign effluence and
inclusiveness, as of the sun, which filled out the place where
he was — yet with something of reserve and sadness in it too,
and a sense of remoteness and inaccessibility."

In person Whitman was impressive. He was six
feet in height, weighed nearly two hundred pounds,

still held himself straight, and was well proportioned. His long, very fine, and nearly snow-white hair and beard made him appear at first sight older than he was, and at sixty he was taken to be seventy or eighty. He walked feebly, owing to his paralysis, but his face had none of the lines of age or weariness. His complexion was singularly ruddy — a bright maroon tint, strikingly in contrast with the whiteness of his hair and beard; and his flesh had a delicate rose colour. Edward Carpenter records that he was "most struck, in his face, by the high arch of the eyebrows, giving a touch of child-like wonder and contemplation to his expression; yet his eyes, though full of a kind of wistful tenderness, were essentially not contemplative but perceptive — active rather than receptive — lying far back, steady, clear, with small definite pupils and heavy lids of passion and experience. A face of majestic simple proportion, like a Greek temple as some one has said; the nose Greek in outline, straight (but not at all thin or narrow, rather the contrary), broad between the brows, and meeting the line of the forehead without any great change of direction; the forehead high, with horizontal furrows, but not excessively high; the head domed, and rising to a great height in the middle, above the ears — not projecting behind; ears large and finely formed; mouth full, but almost quite concealed by hair. A head altogether impressing one by its height, and by a certain untamed 'wild hawk' look, not uncommon among the Americans."

His dress was plain and comfortable. He preferred clothes of light gray, loosely cut, and an overcoat with pockets in the breast cut diagonally, into which he could thrust his hands. He wore a large, soft gray felt hat, usually pushed back on his forehead. His shirts were made to suit his own fancy, with loose, turned-down collars, the neck button several inches lower than usual, and he wore no tie, so that they lay open about his throat and the upper part of his breast. The cuffs sometimes turned up over the coat-sleeves, and the whole impression was one of white and gray and pink.

His manners were informal and unaffected. Introductions meant little. Once he held out his hand (either the left or the right, as chance directed), and grasped that of another, the ceremony was over, and a friendship was begun. His dominant mood, though probably with some exaggeration, was admirably analyzed by Dr. Bucke, who added the perceptions of a skilled physician to the affectionate interest of a friend, in a passage that must be quoted almost in full : —

" His favorite occupation seemed to be strolling or sauntering about outdoors by himself, looking at the grass, the trees, the flowers, the vistas of light, the varying aspects of the sky, and listening to the birds, the crickets, the tree frogs, and all the hundreds of natural sounds. It was evident that these things gave him a pleasure far beyond what they give to ordinary people. . . . Until I knew the man, it had not occurred to me that any one could derive so much absolute happiness from these things as he did. He was very fond of flowers, either wild or cultivated ; liked all sorts. I think he admired lilacs and sunflowers just as much as roses. Perhaps, indeed, no man who ever lived liked so many things and disliked so few as Walt Whitman. All natural objects seemed to have a charm for him. All sights and sounds seemed to please him. He appeared to like (and I believe he did like) all the men, women, and children he saw (though I never knew him to say that he liked any one), but each who knew him felt that he liked him or her, and that he

liked others also.   I never knew him to argue or dispute, and he
never spoke about money.   He always justified, sometimes
playfully, sometimes quite seriously, those who spoke harshly
of himself or his writings, and I often thought he took pleasure in
the opposition of enemies.   When I first knew him, I used to
think that he watched himself, and would not allow his tongue
to give expression to fretfulness, antipathy, complaint, and
remonstrance.   It did not occur to me as possible that these
mental states could be absent in him.   After long observation,
however, I satisfied myself that such absence or unconscious-
ness was entirely real.   He never spoke deprecatingly of any
nationality or class of men, or time in the world's history, or
against any trades or occupations — not even against any animals, insects, or inanimate things, nor any of the laws of
nature, nor any of the results of those laws, such as illness,
deformity, and death.   He never complained or grumbled
either at the weather, pain, illness, or anything else.   He never
swore.   He could not very well, since he never spoke in anger
and apparently never was angry.   He never exhibited fear, and
I do not believe he ever felt it."

This Saint Martin's summer of his later life Whitman expressed rather in prose than in verse.   Once
he felt the flush of renewed vigour, he began again his
note-taking and memorandum-making.   Some of these
notes and memoranda, collected in *Specimen Days*,
show how keen was his enjoyment of Nature, now that
he was at last freed from the tyranny of bed and
chair and four walls.   They had less than ever before
to do with men and women.   His thoughts were of
birds and bumblebees, of flowers and trees, of the
scent of the woods and fields, of brooks, and country
lanes, of starlight, of the ice on the Delaware of a
winter's night, of his old mistress, the sea, the image
and sound of whose pounding waves had from boyhood haunted his memory.   They run the whole

gamut of the seasons from sap to frost and back to sap again. They are full of sights and sounds and odours, the accurate record of his sensations. There is little of mood, of subjective shaping of Nature to his own purposes. Rather is his attitude that of cheerful receptivity; one of drawing nearer, as it were, and listening and waiting, of expectancy for he knew not what, until Nature seemed to be actually permeating him with unknown influences. "I had," he records in a parenthesis, "a sort of dream-trance the other day, in which I saw my favorite trees step out and promenade up, down and around, very curiously — with a whisper from one, leaning down as he pass'd me, *We do all this on the present occasion, exceptionally, just for you.*"

Between the country and the city he now passed with more freedom, staying as he chose at Whitehorse with the Staffords, with his brother at Camden, or in Philadelphia at the house of Mrs. Gilchrist. In the autumn of 1876 he made frequent visits to the exposition in Philadelphia. In January, 1877, he spoke in Philadelphia on the one hundred and fortieth anniversary of Thomas Paine's birthday. In February he came to New York, where a reception given in his honour showed him how greatly respect and affection for him had grown among persons of repute. He visited, too, with delight the scenes dear to him in New York, and then went up the Hudson to tarry for a while with Mr. Burroughs amid the beautiful scenery of Ulster County. In 1878 he repeated the excursion, and in the autumn of 1879 he was ready for a longer adventure. In September he journeyed with friends as far west as Colorado, revelling in

enjoyment of the extraordinary beauty of the scenery,
the fertility of the soil, the exuberant vitality of the
cities, and in the pressing realization that these are
new lands in which humanity, untrammelled by much
that oppressed it in older soils, may, if it will, reach a
larger and finer growth.   And such a new people should
have its new literature, he dreamed, one free from all the
accumulated stock phrases and types and situations : —

" Will the day ever come — no matter how long deferr'd —
when those models and lay-figures from the British islands —
and even the precious traditions of the classics — will be reminiscences, studies only ?   The pure breath, primitiveness, boundless prodigality and amplitude, strange mixture of delicacy and
power, of continence, of real and ideal, and of all original and
first-class elements, of these prairies, the Rocky mountains,
and of the Mississippi and Missouri rivers — will they ever
appear in, and in some sort form a standard for our poetry
and art ? "

He was, however, it may be added, disappointed in
one respect.   By his theory, and Plato's, a state's ro-
bustness depended upon the women who would bear
and nurture the young, giving them strong bodies and
healthy minds.   But he was moved to record his as-
tonishment that, while Western women were fashionably dressed and bore themselves well, they did not
seem to " have, either in physique or the mentality
appropriate to them, any high native originality of
spirit or body (as the men certainly have, appropriate to them).   They are ' intellectual ' and fashionable, but dyspeptic-looking and generally doll-like ;
their ambition evidently is to copy their eastern
sisters.   Something far different and in advance must
appear, to tally and complete the superb masculinity
of the West, and maintain and continue it."

In general, he felt himself at home in the West,
particularly at Denver, and wholly in sympathy with
the active and optimistic tone of Western life, a radi-
cally American tone. Indeed, even in the magnificent and turbulent scenery of the high-coloured, irregular cañons he saw a landscape akin to his own
verse : —

" ' I have found the law of my own poems,' was the unspoken
but more-and-more decided feeling that came to me as I pass'd,
hour after hour, amid all this grim yet joyous elemental abandon — this plenitude of material, entire absence of art, untram-
mel'd play of primitive Nature — the chasm, the gorge, the
crystal mountain stream, repeated scores, hundreds of miles —
the broad handling and absolute uncrampedness — the fantastic
forms, bathed in transparent browns, faint reds and grays,
towering sometimes a thousand, sometimes two or three thousand feet high — at their tops now and then huge masses pois'd,
and mixing with the clouds, with only their outlines, hazed in
misty lilac, visible."

And the same thought he expressed, in 1881, in
Spirit that formed this Scene : —

" Spirit that form'd this scene,
    These tumbled rock-piles grim and red,
    These reckless heaven-ambitious peaks,
    These gorges, turbulent-clear streams, this naked freshness,
    These formless wild arrays, for reasons of their own,
    I know thee, savage spirit — we have communed together,
    Mine too such wild arrays for reasons of their own;
    Was't charged against my chants they had forgotten art ?
    To fuse within themselves its rules precise and delicatesse ?
    The lyrist's measur'd beat, the wrought-out temple's grace —
        column and polish'd arch forgot ?
    But thou that revelest here — spirit that form'd this scene,
    They have remember'd thee."

On his return, Whitman spent several months with his brother Jefferson in St. Louis, enjoying its peculiar fusion of Northern and Southern and native and foreign qualities, its bustling and varied life, and the night views of the Mississippi and the great bridge. In January, 1880, he returned to the East, and in May, with irrepressible ardour, he was off on another long jaunt, this time by way of Niagara to London, Ontario, where he was the guest of Dr. Bucke, and, in company with Dr. Bucke, down the St. Lawrence and up the Saguenay. In this almost equally picturesque and stimulating journey and visit, which lasted from May to September, and which is in part recorded in *Specimen Days* and in the recently published *Diary in Canada*, Whitman showed himself as before a methodical and acute observer. He saw not only the beauties of Nature but the works of man, and everywhere he penetrated the outward shell, divining the essentially human importance of what many a good traveller would scarcely have noticed.

The winter of 1880–1881 Whitman spent at Camden and in the country, but in the spring he began his journeyings again, this time on a smaller scale. In April he visited Boston, delivering there his lecture in commemoration of the death of Lincoln as he had previously done in New York and Philadelphia. It was a new Boston that he found, after an absence of twenty years, larger, busier, more active, less puritanical, and Whitman saw it with new eyes, recognizing the current of conservatism that ran so sturdily beneath the surface. It was, he thought, like " a jolly old Greek city," where people lived happily because wisely, and he admired particularly the essentially

New England type of "fine-looking gray-hair'd
women." He paid a short visit to Longfellow, who
had called on him several years before, and records
in his diary the cordiality of Longfellow's welcome,
adding an admirably appreciative page of criticism
of his work and that of Emerson, Bryant, and Whittier, "the mighty four who stamped this first American century with its birth-marks of poetic literature."
The crowning pleasure of the journey, however, was
seeing Mr. Quincy Shaw's remarkable collection of
Millet's pictures, by which he was greatly impressed,
and in which he must have recognized an analogue, in
many particulars, of his own art, highly emotional in
method and democratic in subject.

The summer of 1881 Whitman spent partly in Glen-
dale, a cross-roads village near Whitehorse, with the
Staffords, who were now keeping a country store, and
partly in visits to his friends, including one, with Mr.
Burroughs, to the old Whitman homestead at West
Hills and other scenes of his boyhood. In August he
was in New York, rediscovering the peculiar charm
and comfort of the city in midsummer, and enjoying
especially the beauties of the upper portion of the
island. Staying with his friends, the Johnstons, at
Mott Haven, he worked a few hours each day on the
definitive edition of the *Leaves of Grass.* One
day in August, too, he took breakfast at Pfaff's new
restaurant, the host, his old friend of ante-bellum
days, welcoming him, and recalling with him the various members of the circle that gathered so regularly
in the dingy Broadway cellar. "And there," he records, "Pfaff and I, sitting opposite each other at the
little table, gave a remembrance to them in a style

they would have themselves fully confirm'd, namely,
big, brimming, fill'd-up champagne-glasses, drain'd in
abstracted silence, very leisurely, to the last drop."

In the "elastic, mellow, Indian-summery" autumn
of 1881 Whitman made his last journey to Boston,
lodging at Bullfinch's, by Bowdoin Square, correcting
the proofs of the *Leaves of Grass*, which was at last
to be issued by a distinguished publishing firm, James
R. Osgood and Company, and spending his spare time in
loitering about the city and visiting old friends.   Mr.
Frank Sanborn, whose trial as an Abolitionist he had
attended, meditating a rescue, in 1861, took him out
to Concord, and there he saw Emerson twice, the
second time dining at his house.   Emerson was at
that time not wholly in command of his faculties, and
quite probably he did not always remember Whitman;
he sat for the most part silent, smiling, with his
habitual expression of sweetness, "and the old clear-
peering aspect quite the same."   To Whitman it was
something like a benediction, as he remarked to his
friends, and one can understand the feeling, for he
had kept much of his youthful reverence for Emerson, and he must have been moved by the thought
that he was ending his own career with the blessing
of one who had saluted him so bravely at its beginning.   He was taking his fill of life for the last
time, with keener pleasure than ever.   Old friends
and old scenes seemed doubly dear.   In his diary
he records that "perhaps the best is always cumula-
tive."   The best does not reveal itself at first, "sometimes suddenly bursting forth, or stealthily opening
to me, perhaps after years of unwitting familiarity,
unappreciation, usage."

The second Boston edition, like the first, was ill-fated. Some two thousand copies had been sold when complaint was lodged against it in the office of the attorney-general of Massachusetts by the Society for the Suppression of Vice in Boston. The District Attorney, apparently without close examination of the points at issue, thereupon notified the publishers that the volume fell within the provisions of the public statutes respecting obscene literature. The publishers, who had approved the manuscript and had taken the volume on the express understanding that the poems about which discussion had previously arisen should be printed without change, now felt alarmed, shrinking timorously from the thought of a trial on such a charge. Whitman was willing to do whatever he could to help them out of the difficulty and agreed to make various minor changes, but the attorney-general's office insisted on more extensive alterations, and the publishers decided to drop the book. In lieu of royalty they gave Whitman a clear title to the electrotype plates, and these he put into the hands of a Philadelphia publisher (Rees, Welsh and Company, soon succeeded by David McKay), who sold in a single day an edition of three thousand copies, and soon brought out another edition. No complaint was brought against the book in Pennsylvania, somewhat to the disappointment of the publisher, who would willingly have had the book advertised in that way, and the postmaster at Boston, who had excluded the volume from the mails, was forced to abandon his position on directions from his superior officers. And thus, with the growing intelligence of the country in matters of literature, came to naught the last attempt at public prosecution of Whitman's work.

The remainder of 1882 and the whole of 1883 Whitman passed without notable incident, save the publication in 1882 of *Specimen Days and Collect*, containing all his prose works, and the appearance in 1883 of Dr. Bucke's biography. In 1884, however, a new period of his life began with his removal, March 26, to a house of his own, on Mickle Street, Camden. It was a humble two-story cottage, such as might have been occupied by any working-man in good circumstances, and Whitman bought it for about two thousand dollars, of which sum he had more than half in hand; the remainder was lent him by a generous Philadelphia merchant. Mickle Street was well shaded and fairly broad, and inhabited by the kind of people Whitman felt most at home with. His friends with more delicate tastes found the neighbourhood too common, the street too noisy, the domestic arrangements too simple; and they were at times offended by the odours from a guano factory across the river. But such things meant little or nothing to Whitman; and he soon made himself thoroughly comfortable. For a while an elderly working-man and his wife kept the house for him; but soon their place was taken by a competent widow, Mrs. Mary Davis, who served him until his death with complete fidelity.

The front room downstairs was a sort of office and an antechamber for the reception of callers, and contained the unsold copies of such editions of his books as were not handled by his Philadelphia publishers. His real dwelling-place was a large room above, only

partly carpeted, and heated by a little stove. Its
contents have been described in detail by an English
visitor, Dr. Johnston : —

"All around him were books, manuscripts, letters, papers,
magazines, parcels tied up with bits of string, photographs, and
literary *materiel*, which was piled on the table a yard high,
filled two or three wastepaper baskets, flowed over them on to
the floor, beneath the table, on to and under the chairs, bed,
washstand, etc., so that whenever he moved from his chair he
had literally to wade through this sea of chaotic disorder and
confusion. And yet it was no disorder to him, for he knew where
to lay his hands upon whatever he wanted, in a few moments.

"His apartment is roomy, almost square, with three windows — one blinded up — facing the north. The boarded floor
is partly carpeted, and on the east side stands an iron stove
with stove pipe partly in the room. On the top of the stove is
a little tin mug. Opposite the stove is a large wooden bed-
stead, over the head of which hang portraits of his father and
mother. Near the bed, under the blinded-up window, is the
washstand, a plain wooden one, with a white wash-jug and
basin. There are two large tables in the room, one between
the stove and the window, and one between that and the washstand. Both of these are piled up with all sorts of paper,
scissorings, proof-sheets, books, etc., etc. Some big boxes and
a few chairs complete the furniture. On the walls, and on the
mantel piece, are pinned or tacked various pictures and photographs. He himself sits between the two windows, with his
back to the stove, in the huge cane chair."

In this frugal, comfortable, and characteristic manner Whitman passed the remaining years of his life.
Living as a working-man and among working-men, he
was rich in acquaintances and friendships with that
part of the community, young and old. Men stopped
to chat with him as he sat in front of his door, the
children played about him, and he saw to it that the
sick and the unfortunate shared what prosperity was

his. For drivers in Philadelphia he had a special fondness and, as the agent of others of larger means, he took pleasure in seeing that they did not lack stout gloves and warm coats. But his relations were by no means confined to working-men and their families. He was a welcome and honoured guest at the houses of several well-to-do Philadelphians; his old friends O'Connor, Burroughs, Bucke, came often to see him; and, most important of all, a little band of new friends from Camden itself, chief among whom were Mr. Traubel and Mr. Harned, were gathering about him, — a group of younger disciples, who considered themselves as his bodyguard.   And there were hosts of visitors from abroad and at home, distinguished travellers with letters of introduction, simpler men and women who loved his work and wanted to press his hand for an instant, besides the crowd of mere autograph seekers and cranks. He was impatient with the notoriety hunter, or the extremist of any kind; but the gentle-mannered, open-minded visitor he received cordially, whatever his status might be in the world; such men became at once his friends.   Indeed, the spontaneity of his comradeship was such that formal introduction was not necessary ; names and titles counted for nothing ; whether one had known him for years or was seeing him for the first time was a matter of indifference; he cared not. A complete stranger, in a sympathetic account of a first visit to him, relates that he found him sitting in the open air. After a quick glance Whitman welcomed him with cordiality and began to talk freely and affectionately, and when he rose to go, said, " Come again, son. You come so rarely." One is reminded of Orientals so high

in caste that caste becomes meaningless, so deep in the
secrets of life that distinctions fade away, and all
men are to them really brothers.

The royalties on Whitman's books were not large,
and seemed to be dwindling, so that his income from
such sources was irregular and at times scarcely sufficient even for his simple needs. But now and then
some of his new verses appeared in periodicals and
were well paid for, and he was for years kept on the
staff of the New York *Herald*, receiving a small but
regular remittance, and furnishing verses as he felt
inclined. His friends, too, were always trying to aid
him in one way or another. In 1886, his English
friends collected for him a fund of about a hundred
pounds and in the following year his Boston friends
sent him eight hundred dollars, intended at first to
provide for a cottage at Timber Creek. In the same
year, his friends in New York and Philadelphia arranged for him to give his Lincoln lecture again in
each city, before a distinguished audience, and under
circumstances that brought him considerable sums.
His new friends in Camden took on themselves many
expenses connected with his illness, and whenever any
special need arose in his later life, it had only to reach
the ears or eyes of any of his friends for some one's
purse to be opened at once. As Mr. Donaldson states
in his excellent volume of reminiscences, " there was
after 1882 a settled determination in the United States
that Mr. Whitman should not want for the essentials
of a good livelihood, and this was faithfully seen to."
All these favours he took gratefully, with the grace of
a man who had always paid his way, but who in his
old age was willing to receive from his friends what

M

he would, in other circumstances, have been glad to give. Prudently setting aside whatever he did not at the moment need for himself or for the expenses of his youngest brother, of which he had for years borne half, he was able to accumulate a little fund that would have secured him against want or disaster in any great emergency, and that provided for the future of his brother and paid for the granite tomb which he had built, and in which he desired that his bones should rest, together with those of his father and mother.

The habit of composition was deeply ingrained in Whitman; it may almost be said that he did not stop writing until he stopped living, though the volume of his production (and to some degree its value) gradually diminished as his physical force abated. In 1888, while still very ill, he saw through the press his *November Boughs*, containing a score or more of new poems, together with a considerable amount of prose, — in particular, articles on Elias Hicks and George Fox, both of whom, as men led by the inner light and the inner voice, seemed to him to be his spiritual kinsmen. In 1891, at the very verge of life, he published a few further poems with the pathetic title, *Good-bye, my Fancy !* The closing poem, which gave the name to the volume, has a touch (perhaps a reminiscence) of the *animula vagula, blandula :* —

" Good-bye, my Fancy !
Farewell, dear mate, dear love !
I'm going away, I know not where,
Or to what fortune, or whether I may ever see you again,
So Good-bye, my Fancy.

" Now for my last — let me look back a moment ;
The slower fainter ticking of the clock is in me,
Exit, nightfall, and soon the heart-thud stopping.

Long have we lived, joy'd, caress'd together ;
Delightful ! — now separation — Good-bye, my **Fancy.**

" Yet let me not be too hasty,
Long indeed have we lived, slept, filter'd, become really
blended into one ;
Then if we die we die together, (yes, we'll remain one,)
If we go anywhere we'll go together to meet what happens,
May-be we'll be better off and blither, and learn something,
May-be it is yourself now really ushering me to the true
songs, (who knows?)
May-be it is you the mortal knob really undoing, turning — so
now finally,
Good-bye — and hail ! my Fancy."

But he had still another little handful ready before
his death, which his executors, Dr. Bucke, Mr. Traubel,
and Mr. Harned, issued under the title, chosen by
Whitman himself, of *Old Age Echoes.* One of these
poems, *A Thought of Columbus,* now printed at the end
of the definitive edition of *Leaves of Grass,* was his last
deliberate composition.

As a helper on the mechanical side in the preparation of *November Boughs* and his last literary work,
and as his devoted and unselfish friend, Whitman was
fortunate in having Mr. Horace Traubel, whom he
loved as a grandson, and who encompassed him with
all manner of affectionate solicitude. And it is to Mr.
Traubel, moreover, that the world is indebted for the
publication of parts of a diary which he kept for years,
setting down therein with great detail the record of
his daily intercourse with Whitman. Pressed by the
questions of this young and ardent disciple, the veteran
told bit by bit the long story of his tenacious struggle
for his creed against the allied forces of conventional-
ity, giving fitting honour to those who had early or late

joined his ranks, and pointing out each vantage gained as, decade after decade, the conflict wore on. The *Leaves of Grass* had come in his eyes to be more than a book : it was an attitude toward life, a test of liberality of mind and democratic feeling, almost a doctrine. In all this, however, there was nothing immodest, no touch of the complacent braggart, but rather the honest delight of a very old man in the fact that his vision of the world as love was no longer rejected by all men.

Mr. Traubel has recorded, too, Whitman's passing judgments, delivered in their intimate conversation, without rancour but without reserve, on his literary contemporaries. These were always trenchant, and sometimes seem unduly severe. It must be remembered, however, that Whitman had consistently held himself aloof from the literary guild and from what might be called the literary or educated or cultivated class. Like many men who have toiled with their hands and lived frugally with those who toil, he had at the bottom of his heart a mistrust for the gentleman *per se*, the person who dresses according to his tailor's code, thinks in terms of the code of the schools, and conforms to the elaborate conventions of society. Similarly, he was unfriendly to what he called the West Point way of taking literature, the martinets' fashion, as if it were a matter of technique, of precedents and tradition. " Style " reminded him of artificial flowers. And men of this alien class, men who had at their pleasure accepted his work with limitations and reservations or rejected it entirely, were in their turn accepted by him, at his pleasure, with his own reservations, or rejected entirely. Professors and preachers and philosophers, in particular, all those who give

assent only after due deliberation, after checking their
emotion by their logic, — these he valued less highly
than such as yielded themselves freely, without analysis,
to the promptings of the spirit within them. It is too
early to evaluate such criticism ; but he spoke with
the voice of Demos, and the voice of Demos is very
often that of posterity.

Whitman's vital force failed gradually, but in 1885
he suffered a slight sunstroke, and this marked the close
of his last period of roving and the beginning of closer
confinement. As walking now became more difficult
for him, his closer friends planned a fund to buy him
an easy-riding buggy and a good horse. The older
men of letters throughout the country took their share
in this gladly, and their thoughtful coöperation in such
a timely gift delighted Whitman no less than the gift
itself. Thenceforward he drove regularly and frequently — and, it must be added, often at a speed
somewhat unbecoming his years, having exchanged
the safe beast presented to him for one of a livelier
gait. Only rarely, in these later years, did he leave
Camden or Philadelphia, but in 1887 he read his
Lincoln lecture at the Madison Square Theatre, and
afterward met his friends at a reception at the Westminster Hotel. In June, 1888, just after his sixty-
ninth birthday, he was driving by the Delaware at sunset. The scene was one of unusual splendour and he
urged his horse out into the shallow river, and there,
in contemplation of the sky and the water, spent " an
unspeakable hour," as he described it, of ecstasy. The
evening air chilled him, however, and he suffered several slight attacks of paralysis, for the first time losing
temporarily the power of speech. For some days it

did not seem possible that he could recover, but his
dogged persistency of will brought him back to life
again, and allowed him, by working for short periods,
to see *November Boughs* through the press in his usual
painstaking fashion.

During the winter of 1888–1889 he was virtually a
prisoner, and sat by the fire in his big arm-chair. The
horse and buggy were now sold, and he moved about
on the arm of his nurse, Warren Fritzinger, Mrs. Davis's
son, or in an invalid's chair. At the end of May he
sat for a while at the great dinner given in his honour
on his birthday, a quasi-public function in the largest
hall in Camden. The succeeding winter passed in the
same fashion, but in February, 1890, he read his Lincoln
lecture for the last time before an audience in Camden,
and on his birthday he attended a dinner in his
honour in Philadelphia, at the close of which Colonel
Ingersoll spoke long and eloquently in his praise. In
October, Mr. Ingersoll spoke on the same topic before
a large audience in Philadelphia, and Whitman sat on
the platform, taking the praises showered on him with
the unaffected pleasure of the old man who looks back
on the exploits of his earlier life almost as on those of
another person ; though he thought there was too much
" guff and taffy," he knew that it sprang from good-will
and affection.

The winter of 1890–1891 was one of confinement and
illness. " The main abutments and dikes," he said,
were now " shattered and threatening to give out."
The poems in *Good-bye, my Fancy*, which was published late in 1891, he spoke of as his " last chirps."
" In fact," he said in the preface, " here I am these
current years 1890 and '91, (each successive fortnight

getting stiffer and stuck deeper) much like some hard-
cased dilapidated grim ancient shell-fish or time-bang'd
conch (no legs, utterly non-locomotive) cast up high
and dry on the shore-sands, helpless to move anywhere — nothing left but behave myself quiet, and
while away the days yet assign'd, and discover if there
is anything for the said grim and time-bang'd conch to
be got at last out of inherited good spirits and primal
buoyant centre-pulses down there deep somewhere
within his gray-blurr'd old shell." Slowly he grew
more frail and more feeble, and his hoary head, resting
on the wolfskin in the heavy old chair, was like that
of an aged prophet. But he was present at his last
birthday dinner, given in his house, and bore himself
with gayety. Still he kept busy, so far as his strength
allowed, with reading and writing, but he was notice-
ably more silent, sitting for hours in quiet meditation.

In 1891 the gray granite tomb was completed, and
the ashes of his father and mother transported thither.
All was ready for its other occupant, and he did not
long tarry. The consulting physician who examined
him early in the year found no evidence of gross
organic disease, but recorded that his apparent age
was greater than his real years. He complained of
" torpor inertia — as though a great wet soggy net
were spread over me and holding me down." His own
diagnosis was interesting : " possibly," he wrote to the
physician, " that slow, vital, almost impalpable by-play
of automatic stimulus belonging to living fibre has, by
gradual habit of years and years in me (and especially of the last three years), got quite diverted into
mental play and vitality and muscular use." In other
words the mind was ceasing to inform the body and

recoiling upon itself. The physician agreed with him
that there might be a great deal in the hypothesis;
but the post-mortem examination showed that deep-
seated pathological processes were at that time going
on. Almost to the end of the year he kept up his
mental activity. "Never idle," notes Dr. Longaker,
"he sat surrounded by a vast heap of books, papers,
manuscripts, and what not, always busied in something." On December 17 a sharp chill presaged the
setting in of pneumonia. Soon very little of the lung
surface was active, and his spirit seemed on the
point of departure, but his stubborn vitality rallied,
and he lived for nearly three months. He still insisted each day on reading the papers, and he sent
messages, and wrote short notes, and did not until the
end lose hold entirely of the actual world, though he
lay for hours in a state of acute quiescence, with all
his senses active but turned inward, so to speak. He
suffered acutely and constantly, slept little and restlessly, and became greatly emaciated, but kept his
characteristic charm and cheerfulness. At last, on
March 26, the exhausted vital flame flickered and
then went out. The physicians who made the post-
mortem examination thought it marvellous that he
could have lived so long. "It was no doubt due largely
to that indomitable will pertaining to Walt Whitman.
Another would have died much earlier with one-half
of the pathological changes that existed in his body."

On March 30, the little cottage was, for some hours,
open to the procession of thousands who wished to
look once more upon his face. Many had come from
afar, but the great mass were the people of the town,
working-men and women and children. In the after-

noon the funeral services were held in the open air, in the presence of a multitude, at the cemetery. His older and nearer friends made brief addresses, and one of them read passages from the sacred writings of various peoples, all expressing belief in the immortality of the soul. There was little mourning for the poet and seer who had lived to the term of his natural years, but rather joy in his love and thankfulness for his influence. To those who might be called his disciples, it was a day of heightened, joyful emotion. " We are at the summit," said one. Their great leader had fulfilled his earthly mission.

A short biography has no room for critical analysis, nor is it its function to provide it, particularly when the subject is a writer so near to us in point of time. Generations must pass before opinion hardens and unifies. It may not be too early, however, to guess at the present trend in the estimate of Whitman's poetry. In the years immediately following the publication of *Leaves of Grass*, his contemporaries were much exercised over elements in his work that do not now attract great attention. Then they were bewildered by his form of free verse; now the boundaries of taste and appreciation have been much enlarged, and our increasing acquaintance with Oriental poetry and the general movement toward free verse in English and in other literatures have greatly diminished the prejudice. Whitman's rhymeless and faintly rhythmical form seems less and less an innovation and more and more to be merely one of the many known ways of producing poetic effects. Then the public was startled by the degree to which he stressed

the facts of sex. Now we are less inclined to dogma-
tism on the content of poetry, and in any event we
understand that Whitman's seeming insistence in such
matters was connected with his larger theory of the
ideal state and, further, that the emphasis of the
greater part of his work falls elsewhere. Then critics
found his personality turbulent and egotistic : the bar-
baric yaup that he sounded over the roofs of the
world was thought to be his own braggart voice.
Now we see that he spoke as the symbol of democracy.

There remains only one element of Whitman's verse
to which the public at large is still somewhat unfriendly — his multitudinous inventories and catalogues, and about this point the critics are still at vari-
ance. It begins to grow clearer, however, that this
element is of the very essence of his art ; that it was
perhaps actually the origin of his art. It was, I surmise, through the psychological process of which the inventory is the sign that he reached the peculiar state of
consciousness by virtue of which he is a poet ; and the
inventory is the test of the reader's ability to follow
him in this process. Whoever would have the mystic's
poetic illusion must use the mystic's means. If this
be true, it follows that this special method has limited
very considerably the general appreciation of Whitman's poetry. From this point of view, as from others,
Whitman may perhaps be best regarded as a forerunner. The peculiarly cosmic quality of his verse, its
power of unifying details infinite in number and heter-
ogeneous in character, is due to the method of expression which he devised ; but the method reveals
his great vision only to a few. Possibly, as time

wears on, there will come others, stimulated by him
to embrace the whole framework of the world in their
sympathy, who will discover a medium less mystical,
more intellectual, which will not prove such a barrier.
Or, perhaps, the unities of the universe will never
be grasped save in the mystic's vision, and never expressed in verse save for those that can follow his
steps at a great distance.

   Nor have we space for an extended treatment of
Whitman's literary relationships — of the writers that
influenced him and the writers whom he has influenced.   Fortunately, such an inquiry is not of great
importance in Whitman's case.   He was little influenced by books.   When his mind was simmering,
as he once said, Emerson helped to bring it to a boil ;
but he was never a man of books, and so far as his
ideas were conditioned by those of others it was
rather by the whole widely diffused spirit of American, English, and German transcendentalism than by
any particular work or author.   His influence on other
writers has been somewhat more marked, and can be
traced in several literatures.   But the new form in
which he cast his expression was one of which he
alone held the delicate secret.   No one else has
succeeded in mastering it, and his influence has
tended to blend and assimilate itself with all the
cognate forces that lead to the expression of similar
ideas in free verse.

   Whitman has been often likened to Rousseau, to
Carlyle, to Browning, to Tolstoi, and to Nietsche, and
there are obvious similarities in each case.   The
points of dissimilarity, however, are even more strik-

ing. Rousseau was less robust; Carlyle, less positive
in his influence; Browning, more analytic and intellectual; Nietsche, more insurgent and rebellious;
Tolstoi, more ascetic and conscience-haunted. Whitman's analogues, I suspect, are rather to be found
in great personalities, in men who represent a
new attitude, in men who bring a message to their
brothers, a truth mainly expressed in their lives
and only incidentally through their writings, — such
men, shall we say, as Francis of Assisi, or George
Fox, or many an Oriental teacher of earlier or later
times. These are the great accepters and unifiers of
life; their teachings and examples pass beyond the
confines of literature or politics; they show new and
noble ways of living. Of this type, in his own degree,
Whitman seems to me to have been. He is the first
and the most notable of those who, in the nineteenth
century, in Europe and in America, preached the
vision of the world as love and comradeship.

INDEX

Alcott, Bronson, 76.
American Primer, 79.
Arnold, Matthew, 111.
Ashton, J. H., 107, 129.

Beecher, H. W., 76.
Björnson, 135.
Blake, 41.
Browning, Robert, 171.
Bryant, 76, 155.
Buchanan, Robert, 143.
Bucke, R. M., 7, 8, 13, 23, 52, 94, 96, 116, 146, 149, 154, 160, 163.
Burroughs, John, 7, 63, 76, 96, 113, 129, 151, 155, 160.

Calamus, 116.
Carlyle, 62, 66, 122, 125, 171.
Carpenter, Edward, 147.
Chase, S. P., 106.
Conway, M. D., 76.

Dana, C. A., 75.
Davis, Mrs. Mary, 158, 166.
Democratic Vistas, 121, 127.
Diary in Canada, 154.
Donaldson, Thomas, 161.
Dowden, Edward, 133, 135.
Doyle, Peter, 114, 128, 129, 140, 141.
Drum-taps, 98.

Eldridge, C. W., 83, 91, 96, 98, 129.
Emerson, 36, 43, 47, 62, 65, 73, 84, 106, 155, 156, 171.

Fox, George, 162, 172.
Francis of Assisi, 172.

Franklin Evans, 18, 28.
Freiligrath, Ferdinand, 132.
Fritzinger, Warren, 166.

Gilchrist, Mrs. Anne, 135, 136, 151.
Good Gray Poet, The, 108.

Hale, E. E., 64.
Harlan, James, 107.
Harned, T. B., 160, 163.
Hawthorne, 28.
Hicks, Elias, 17, 162.
Holmes, 47.
Houghton, Lord, 76.
Howells, W. D., 77.

Ingersoll, R. G., 166.

James, William, 50, 53.
Johnston, Dr. John, 159.
Johnston, J. H., 155.

Leaves of Grass, first appearance, 56; summary of, 57–60; sale, 61; reception, 61–65; approval of Emerson, 65; W.'s reviews of, 67; second edition, 75; third edition, Boston, 83; fifth edition, 119; summary of, 119–122; English edition, selections, 134; sixth edition, 142.
Longfellow, 36, 47, 155.
Lowell, 47, 51, 85.

Memoranda of the War, 144.
Myers, F. W., 132.

173